CUT THESE WORDS INTO MY STONE

Also by Michael Wolfe

Verse

How Love Gets Around, 1974

World Your Own, 1976

No, You Wore Red, 1980

Paradise: Reading Notes, 2010

Greek to Me, 2012

Travel

In Morocco, 1980

The Hadj: An American's Pilgrimage to Mecca, 1993

One Thousand Roads to Mecca, 1997

Essays

Taking Back Islam, 2003

CUT THESE WORDS INTO MY STONE

Ancient Greek Epitaphs

Translated by
Michael Wolfe

Foreword by
Richard P. Martin

The Johns Hopkins University Press
Baltimore

Printed in the United States of America on acid-free paper
2 4 6 8 9 7 5 3 1

The Johns Hopkins University Press
2715 North Charles Street
Baltimore, Maryland 21218-4363
www.press.jhu.edu

Library of Congress Cataloging-in-Publication Data

Wolfe, Michael, 1945–
Cut these words into my stone : ancient Greek epitaphs / translated by Michael Wolfe; foreword by Richard P. Martin
pages. cm.
Includes bibliographical references.
ISBN 978-1-4214-0803-3 (hdbk. : alk. paper) – ISBN 978-1-4214-0804-0 (pbk. : alk. paper) – ISBN 978-1-4214-0805-7 (electronic) – ISBN 1-4214-0803-1 (hdbk. : alk. paper) – ISBN 1-4214-0804-X (pbk. : alk. paper) – ISBN 1-4214-0805-8 (electronic)
1. Epitaphs – Greece. I. Title.
CN375.E6W65 2013
929′.5–dc23
2012020457

A catalog record for this book is available from the British Library.

Special discounts are available for bulk purchases of this book. For more information, please contact Special Sales at 410-516-6936 or specialsales@press.jhu.edu.

The Johns Hopkins University Press uses environmentally friendly book materials, including recycled text paper that is composed of at least 30 percent post-consumer waste, whenever possible.

For my tutors in Greek over the years
Dudley Fitts and Kevin Whitfield and Andy Gaus

In Memoriam
Violet Fosdick and David Wolfe
Tekla Fosdick and Harry Grace
Holly Grace Spivak
Catherine and Frank Summa

CONTENTS

TRANSLATOR'S NOTE

This book offers the reader a chronological selection of ancient Greek epitaphs in new English translations, along with the originals and just enough commentary to appreciate their context.

The earliest surviving epitaphs in Greek date to the mid-700s BCE and represent some of Europe's oldest writing. Those collected here span a period from about 500 BCE to around 600 CE. Greek epitaphs continued to be written long after that, but never again so well. Notable developments in the form occurred over time. The book divides 127 epitaphs into five periods reflecting that evolution.

The pieces here come mainly from the Greek Anthology, Book 7, along with certain ones from Books 9 and 11 and a few from other sources. The commentaries of A. S. F. Gow and D. L. Page have been useful in finding English equivalents for particular words and lines. Almost all of these versions were submitted over several years to the cautious eye of Andy Gaus, a gifted translator. Thanks are also due to Danilo Piana, for helpful comments in the final stages of preparation.

Greek epitaphs have often been translated into other languages, beginning with Classical Latin. In English, their memorable ring is echoed in the works of seventeenth-century Cavalier poets like Robert Herrick. Alexander Pope, Thomas Gray, William Cowper, Shelley, and Byron all tried their hand at the elegiac epigram, knew its main repository, the Greek Anthology, and translated or echoed its distinctive voice. The Greek epitaph's unique spirit reappears in modern poetry too: A. E. Housman, W. B. Yeats, Edgar Lee Masters, D. H. Lawrence, Ezra Pound, T. S. Eliot, Charles Olson, J. V. Cunningham, Robert Duncan, Richard Wilbur, Robert Creeley, Keith Waldrop, and others have employed its tropes and tone.

Richard P. Martin's adventuresome foreword to this volume tracks the epitaph's origins and development in ways that will engage and inform both general and more specialized readers. Near the back of the book, a brief bibliography lists a few volumes of critical scholarship. They in turn contain more extensive bibliographies. I have included thumbnail biographies of the poets and notes that provide the original source information and add some clarification to certain verses.

In some of the Greek epitaphs, readers may notice the use of the dagger symbol (†). In philology, the dagger, also called an obelisk or *crux desperationis* (cross of despair), is the traditional symbol used by textual critics (philologists) to signal a *locus deperditus* (irreparably lost place), a passage so corrupted by subsequent mistakes in the transmission of a text as to discourage any attempt at restoration.

A few of the translations, sometimes in a slightly different form, originally appeared in the following publications: "Laugh, I Thought I'd Die," in the Phi Beta Kappa Society's *Key Reporter,* Fall 2011; *Paradise: Reading Notes,* Blue Press, 2010; *The North Dakota Review,* Fall 2007; *Uncontained: Writers and Photographers in the Garden and on the Margins, an Anthology,* Jennifer Heath, editor. Baksun Books, 2006.

FOREWORD

Epigrams are literally "inscriptions."* An epitaph, the earliest form of epigram, is an inscription "on a tomb" (*epi-* and *taphos*). In both cases, the name explains the poetic form—its origins and its most striking characteristic, brevity. Verses inscribed on an object, whether a marker for a grave or an offering to the gods, had to be short to fit a limited surface. Practical considerations (the cost of stone or metal, the labor of engraving) had literary consequences. Greek poets learned to exploit the limitations of space, to use this miniature laboratory for experimenting with extreme compression in meaning, allusion, plot, and character. The poems that emerged from this centuries-long development shine diamond-hard, with a brilliant attraction for readers as well as translators. Hence, the gems here.

---

* The Greek compound *epigramma* matches, prefix and stem, its Latin synonym, *in-* and *epi-*, both signaling "on," while the Latin *script-* (from *scribere*, "write") corresponds to Greek *graphein* (yielding, for its part, *gramma*, "letter"—and eventually such scriptural English words as *grammar, telegraph, paragraph,* and *graphite*).

The meter and wording of ancient epigrams are shared to a great extent with the other extreme in Greek poetic production, the grand and very lengthy heroic epics. At first sight, the *Iliad* and *Odyssey* may seem to have little to do with a few inscribed lines on a pot or gravestone. The epics were originally composed in live performance, using a highly refined yet flexible system of set phrases that enabled the oral poet to elaborate and expand any episode as he or she saw fit (or that day's audience demanded). Repetition—of words, motifs, typical scenes and incidents—lay at the heart of this technique. Epic is poetry made for public re-performance. Epigrams, on the other hand, seem designed for private reading, once. Rather than depending on an audience's knowledge of old stories and its desire to hear more, they offer information, to be encountered, considered, and then passed by. If epic is timeless myth, epigram is news. Whereas the archetypal scene of epic performance features a bard who enchants crowds of listeners, that of epigram, and the epitaph in particular, is the vision of a traveler who comes upon a solitary tomb and reads on the gravestone (or is told by it, for some stones "speak") the barest sketch of a person's life.

Yet metrically, epic and epigram differ at most by only three syllables. The hexameter line of Homeric poetry can be represented as six "feet," the first five starting with a long syllable followed by two short ones or another long one. The final foot has two syllables, the last of which is either long or short. Thus, the first line of the *Odyssey* scans:

— ˇ ˇ —ˇˇ — ˇ ˇ — ˇ ˇ — ˇ ˇ —ˇ

Andra moi ennepe Mousa polutropon hos mala polla
Tell me, Muse, of that much-turning man who many
. . .

And so it runs for more than 12,000 lines, each verse slightly different but basically identical, waves rolling onto the hearer's consciousness. In the epigram, this oceanic quality of Homeric poetry is a distant echo. Its standard meter, the "elegiac couplet," appends to each Homeric-style hexameter verse a second line composed of two parts, each comprising two-and-a-half dactyls, with a break between words in the middle, like this:

– ˇ ˇ – ˇ ˇ – ˇ ˇ – ˇ ˇ – ˇ ˇ – x
– ˇ ˇ – ˇ ˇ – // – ˇ ˇ – ˇ ˇ –

In English, if the long and short syllables were replaced by equivalent stresses, the two lines working together would sound like this couplet by the English poet Arthur Hugh Clough:

Come, let us go,–to a land wherein gods of the old
time wandered,
Where every breath even now changes to ether
divine.

The pattern is internally echoic, even reflective, as if through the second line a portion of the first were being turned over in the mind twice. Most often, the second verse concludes a sentence. Thought pauses, and there is the sense of an ending. This makes the single couplet feel appropriate for mention of the dead, a concentrated cry gradually fading into silence:

— — — — —   ˇ ˇ — — —ˇ ˇ —   —

Ê kalon to mnêma [*pa*]*têr estêse thanous*[*êi*]

—ˇ ˇ   — ˇ ˇ— // —ˇ   ˇ—   ˇ   ˇ —

Learetêi. ou gar [*et*]*i*   *zôsan esopsom*[*etha*]

Lovely the tombstone her father set up
To Learete, for we will not see her alive again.

This late sixth-century BC sepulchral poem–epigram as epitaph–from the northern island of Thasos is typical of many that have been found, their writing more or less intact, on sites across the Aegean and mainland Greece. Already in the Archaic period (700–500 BCE) such poems expressed not just the name of the deceased but an attitude, the sentiment of those who mourned. In the example above, the focus on the beautiful object increases the pathos, as the gravestone will never compensate for the loss of the living girl whom it commemorates. Since some inscribed poems originally accompanied life-size statues, the interplay among inscribed stone, absent loved one, and living reader becomes all the more marked. An exquisite archaic *korê* statue in the National Museum in Athens speaks for another dead girl through the epitaph inscribed on its marble base:

Sêma Phrasikleias. Kourê keklêsomai aiei
anti gamou para theôn touto lakhous' onoma.

Phrasikleia's headstone: *I will be called a virgin for all time. This title I won from the gods instead of marriage.*

Ancient Greek poems never rhyme, but epitaphs like these make up for it with rich alliteration and subtly interwoven sound patterns, devices to be exploited in thousands of poems that followed later in the tradition. Homeric epic rarely exhibits such distillations of pure sound, despite its metrical affiliation with the shorter poetic genre.

Beyond the level of form, what unites epic and epitaph is a shared artistic concern: to craft the most memorable evocation of special persons, whether heroes or kin, and to keep their memory alive for the ages. The *Iliad* accomplishes this in verses that would have required several days to perform, while the epitaph takes seconds. Of course, the latter genre was never in competition with the former, nor was epitaph derived from epic—our first evidence for either comes from the same period. It makes better sense to think of the two forms as coexistent and complementary. Attitudes encapsulated in the short poems can summon up the *ethos* of the long compositions—*and* the opposite can also happen. In a striking scene from Book Seven of the *Iliad*, the Homeric poet appears to be already aware of epigrammatic style. He makes the Trojan prince Hector, speaking before his duel with Ajax, promise to return his opponent's corpse, should the Greek hero lose. Then, says the Trojan, the companions of Ajax might heap up a tomb by the Hellespont, so that someday in the future a passing sailor might say: "This is the tomb (*sêma*) of one who died long ago, slain at his moment of glory by shining Hector" (*Il.*7.89–90). The two hexameter lines that Hector places in the mouth of the far distant viewer enshrine his *own* name, as killer, even as they obliterate his enemy's. Except for that aggressive reversal, the lines would make a perfectly good epitaph. In reconstructing such poetic interaction, it helps to recall that many of the earliest inscriptions were in fact composed entirely in hexameters, rather than the elegiac couplets that became universal later.

This scene from the *Iliad* also anticipates a key development that eventually produced the poems you will find translated here: the unlinking of poetic text from the object it actually marks. Hector is quite clearly *not* talking about words on a stone (writing being unknown, it seems, to the composers of the *Iliad*). But he *is* imagining an utterance prompted by a material object—the tomb of Ajax. And indeed, as far as style goes, the imagined verses *could* be inscribed on the very object—so closely do they resemble extant epitaphs on stones. "Imagining what could be inscribed" best summarizes the poetic motivation for the majority of Greek epitaphs. Perhaps this crucial step was enabled by the increasingly widespread use of writing in the Classical period (circa 500–350 BCE). With the development of a reading public, the move from inscribing on stone or pots to "inscribing" a papyrus scroll, while fictionalizing a different material context for the poem, was an interesting possibility for the poets. This adds, moreover, a new dimension to the older dynamic of reading: rather than a one-time viewer reading in public the verses on a stone (reading *aloud* having been the norm in antiquity), now a private reader, far removed from any monument, reenacts, as many times as she chooses, the encounter with a gravestone or dedicated object. In imaginary epitaphs we see the earliest beginnings of virtual reality.

Another contributing factor to the separation of text from object might well have been the custom of the cenotaph (literally "empty tomb"). Greeks traveled far and wide as merchants and traders, colonists and explorers, mercenaries and citizen-soldiers. Not all made their way home. Deaths at sea or on distant shores were commemorated by the deceased's family, without the remains. An epitaph in this collection, although composed centuries later, makes a good example:

> I wish fast ships had never been invented.
> We wouldn't be standing here now
> Mourning Sopolis, Diokleides' son.
>
> His homeless corpse floats lost at sea
> While we bow our heads in passing,
> Not to him—to a name on an empty tomb.

The separation of the object of mourning from the inscribed poem that remembers him provides a parallel for freeing the text from its immediate referent. It is curious, therefore, that Simonides (circa 556–468 BCE) is the earliest writer of epitaphs whom we know by name, for he is also the man credited with crafting the verses for several famous cenotaphs (as well as regular epitaphs) in the time of the Persian Wars. So celebrated did he become for his artistry in this genre that many epigrams were ascribed to him in later antiquity that he almost certainly did not write. It is as if the cenotaph habit, the ability to imagine the separation of object and verses, untethered the poet's own connection to a particular time and place, making him a kind of floating signifier—whatever "Simonides" celebrated was implicitly important. Closer to the actual era of Simonides, only one monument is clearly associated with him by name. The historian Herodotus, born about sixty years later than the poet, tells us that after the battle of Thermopylae in 480 BCE, a coalition of neighboring states commissioned two inscriptions commemorating the Greeks who tried to hold off the Persians at the mountain pass (translated here on pages 32 and 33). The composer is not recorded (although later generations assumed it was Simonides). He is, however, tied explicitly to a third poem that he "inscribed" (or "commissioned") to honor the seer Megistias. The seer, having foretold his own death in the upcoming battle, sent away his son but ultimately refused to leave the side of the Spartan commander Leonidas (see page 31 here). Herodotus tells us that Simonides' praise was the result of his personal friendship with the deceased. Once again, the motif of dislocation seems to mark this pivotal epigrammatist, composing verses for people not there, or for one who could have got away.

Yet another social phenomenon, the symposium, played a crucial role in the development of literary epigrams from inscriptions designed for a particular place and object into widely circulating works of poetic art. This age-old Greek social institution that combined politics, entertainment, and ritual with copious wine drinking seems to have helped the epigram to morph from functional to fictional, growing into the most popular poetic genre of antiquity. Archaeologists note that some of the earliest burial sites of the Iron Age had adjacent areas for dining, so it is probable that at least one variety of the ancient symposium was funereal. Even today, it is Greek custom for the family of the deceased to gather right after a burial for shared drink and food; there are rooms specially designated for this within the Proto Nekrotapheio, the central cemetery of modern Athens. At the ancient events, we can imagine the praises of the dead being recounted and sung. It is not coincidental, then, that the verse-form most closely associated with symposia is none other than the elegiac couplet, identical to the metrical form of most Greek epitaphs. The small inscribed poems might be thought of as snatches of longer commemorative compositions, eulogies perhaps made on the spot. Conversely, an epitaph might be the kernel of a later song—it is difficult to assign priority in the process. What still puzzles scholars is the wide topical range of the longer "elegiac" poems that actually survive in this meter. The earliest examples, from the works of the seventh-century soldier-poet Archilochus, include speeches meant to rouse troops, descriptions of battle and retreat, a prohibition against mourning, and a call for heavy drinking with comrades.

At a symposium, participants could recite or sing elegies, but they might also recount the shorter epigrams seen in their travels or heard from others—or invented. That is to say, the dozens of drinking parties going on in any given night in any of hundreds of Greek city-states functioned as a social network for transmitting—and creating—short poems of this type, even before writing became widespread. The institution of the symposium also helps explain two other characteristics of Greek epitaphs: their themes, often related to love or drink (primary activities at symposia) and the quest for inventiveness on the part of their composers. Performing at parties was clearly a desirable social refinement, as we see from Plato's depictions of late-fifth-century Athenian life, and the nearly contemporary comedies of Aristophanes (e.g., *The Wasps*). We have scraps of at least one songbook from the third-century BCE, apparently a papyrus scroll meant to help a would-be symposiast remember verses on an evening out. If we imagine the pressures for improvisation at such events, the need to find a new twist on the venerable topic of death, we can appreciate anew the tabloid-worthy tales recounted by some "epitaphs," from a woman who meets death as she is undressing for her marriage night (*Anthologia Palatina* [*The Palatine Anthology*] 7.182; page 116 here) to the crew whose boat sank because a flock of cranes alighted on its rigging (7.543, page 113). These nest side by side with epitaphs for victims of less uncommon antique fates: falls down wells, earthquakes, house fires, roof collapses, infant diseases, shipwrecks, wars—and, occasionally, even old age. Nor does the knowledge that by Hellenistic times many of these epitaphs are literary artifacts rather than actual inscriptions prevent one from being moved at the death of a favorite horse (7.208; page 70) or a boy too young to have learned to walk in sandals (7.365, page 118). As always, fictions well-handled make life more real.

If anything unites the thousands of Greek epitaphs, it is the essential Greek trait of loving words. Not only are the inscribed words presented to the individualized dead, like the final libation at a tomb, a fixed form of the living breath to be breathed again when a passer-by recites. There is an unquestioned – though hardly religious – faith in personal *post mortem* existence, so that the dead speak back from their tombs (or, at cenotaphs, from afar). One can even converse with them, the way an anonymous visitor, in an epigram by Callimachus, questions the dead Charidas about conditions in Hades (7.524; page 81). Death, no matter how grim, can be talked back to. A human voice endures, small, wise, and flinty as the Greek landscape itself.

Philology – literally, the "love of words" – designates the arts of preserving, restoring, and interpreting texts. It was philology that ensured survival for these little memorials, even when the stones wore down and the old speech died out. The present collection continues an ancient scholarly habit of anthologizing epigrams and a Renaissance tradition of translating them. Already at the end of the Classical period, the antiquarian Philochorus (circa 340–260 BCE) was transcribing inscriptions that dealt with Athenian history, whether from tombs or temple dedications. Many must have been in verse. A collection of inscriptions from other cities was made about a century later by Polemo, a geographer and student of Stoicism. The crucial work of collecting and arranging these short poems, however, was carried out by poets themselves, starting in the years after the death of Alexander the Great, in the cosmopolitan capital he had established, Alexandria in Egypt. Callimachus, an immensely learned scholar-poet of the first half of the third-century BCE, wrote his own epigrams (brilliant poems, some of them translated here). Although we do not know explicitly that he also collected and edited epigrams, it is recorded that he arranged the works of archaic poets, such as Pindar, and wrote 120 books on the history of Greek literature, even as he catalogued the huge Library of Alexandria. His poetic preferences for brevity, conciseness, irony, and allusion fit perfectly the aesthetic of literary epigrams, and it would be surprising if he was not deeply aware of earlier examples and did not do something to organize them.

A contemporary, Posidippus from Pella in Macedonia, also labored at Alexandria under the patronage of the court of the Ptolemies, the Macedonian successors of Alexander. Well known in antiquity, particularly for his epigrams, he suffered the same fate as Callimachus – only a small portion of his work survives. In 2001, however, the number of probable Posidippan epigrams skyrocketed with the discovery and publication of a papyrus that had been torn up and used to wrap an Egyptian mummy. Of the 112 poems on the papyrus fragments – more than 600 lines of Greek – only two were known before, and they had been attributed to Posidippus, making it likely that the whole of the newly discovered scroll is his. The scroll itself dates from only a few decades after the poet's death, and it is possible that it represents his own arrangement of epigrams, by topic: in the extant portion we find gemstones, winning race horses, and divination through bird signs among the major categories. The "new Posidippus" makes especially clear the way in which epigrams were packaged and transmitted as poetic "books" for a reading public.

Around 100 BCE, Meleager, a poet from Gadara in Syria, living on the Greek island of Kos, crafted a selection from such single-author books (and perhaps other collections), calling his anthology *Stephanus* (*Garland*). This pioneering arrangement does not survive intact. Large portions, however, were copied into later anthologies; at the same time, parts were lost, whether from negligence or changes in taste. Another collection titled *Garland* was produced under the reign of the emperor Nero by the Greek poet Philip of Thessalonica, something of an update and supplement to Meleager's. It included works by Philip, his talented countryman Antipater, and, among others, Philodemus of Gadara (circa 110–40 BCE), the philosopher friend of Roman poets Virgil and Horace. This anthology as well came to be selectively copied into later, larger collections and has been reconstructed by scholars on the basis of such extracts. Philip's *Garland* seems to have added to the eventual mix a number of "epideictic" epigrams—literally "show-off" poems—ranging from the description of art works to fictional epitaphs for Classical writers, invitations to parties, congratulatory verses, and invectives.

The snowballing continued through the long centuries of the Byzantine Empire. Constantine Cephalas, palace chaplain in Constantinople in the early tenth century CE, produced from earlier collections the largest anthology, determining the thematic categories that shaped succeeding collections—sepulchral, dedicatory, descriptive, erotic, satiric, etc. The last wave that brought ancient epigrams to our day stemmed, it appears, from this priest's massive work. It is represented in various ways by two medieval manuscripts. *The Palatine Anthology* (*Anthologia Palatina*) was written later in the tenth century on 710 pages of parchment. The second manuscript on which our knowledge of the earlier collections depends was completed in September 1301, as its editor attests in the autograph copy now in Venice. The writer and theologian Maximus Planudes was Byzantine ambassador to the Venetian Republic. His reshaping of Cephalas contains nearly 400 poems that did not make their way into the Palatine manuscript.

Together, these volumes form the so-called "Greek Anthology." But they do not hold all the Greek epigrams known to the modern world. Dozens of ancient authors, such as Plutarch and Diogenes Laertius, preserve several hundred not in either manuscript. Hundreds more have been found on stones since the rise of organized archaeological exploration in the nineteenth century. No single book contains all these other verses. A small number have been included in the present volume. The bulk of the poems here were transmitted among the 750 poems that make up Book 7 of the Anthology, the section on sepulchral epigrams.

A complete history of translations of the Anthology would make for a long shelf, groaning under large books. It would be much easier to list the writers in English who do *not* owe anything to it. From George Turbervile (*Epitaphes, Epigrams, Songs and Sonets,* 1567) to Alicia Stallings (*Hapax,* 2006), the Greek poems are a part of the English literary landscape, a necessary presence. Michael Wolfe's superb and unshowy translations keep both the intimate quality of voice and the tautness and precision of the Greek. Nothing is prettified, but nothing is made mean. Edgar Lee Masters and Ezra Pound can be counted among progenitors of this style, to name just two Americans deeply influenced by the Anthology. George Seferis and Constantine Cavafy among the modern Greeks, Eugenio Montale and Salvatore Quasimodo in Italy, found their way by different paths to similar re-performances of this poetry, stripped down yet evocative, either in direct translation or in imitations of attitude and tone. Wolfe's versions rank with theirs. That the verses here speak to the twenty-first century prompts amazement, as well as the hope that human wisdom – independent, unadorned, illusionless, wry – might still be heard.

BIBLIOGRAPHICAL NOTE

On the change in Athenian culture from oral to written, see Rosalind Thomas, *Oral Tradition and Written Record in Classical Athens* (Cambridge: Cambridge University Press, 1989). On practices of reading in relation to archaic epigrams, see Jesper Svenbro, *Phrasikleia: An Anthropology of Reading in Ancient Greece,* trans. Janet Lloyd (Ithaca: Cornell University Press, 1993). Poems in verse found as inscriptions are collected and edited (with Greek text and notes, but no translation) in two volumes by P. A. Hansen: *Carmina Epigraphica Graeca Saeculorum VIII–V a. Chr. n.* (Berlin: de Gruyter, 1983) and *Carmina Epigraphica Graeca Saeculi IV a. Chr. n.* (Berlin: de Gruyter, 1989). The history of epigram translation is partially covered by James Hutton's two volumes, *The Greek Anthology in Italy to the Year 1800* (Ithaca: Cornell University Press, 1935) and *The Greek Anthology in France and in the Latin Writers of the Netherlands to the Year 1800* (Ithaca: Cornell University Press, 1946), but much work remains to be done.

CUT THESE WORDS INTO MY STONE

I

Anonymous Epitaphs of No Known Date

Anonymous epitaphs and dedications are among the earliest surviving examples of Greek writing. Rudimentary samples appear concurrently with the invention of the alphabet, in the middle of the eighth century BCE. Chiseled on pillars, incised on votive tablets and funerary pottery, these spare metered memorials, often just one line long, provided the basis for a much later invention, the literary epigram. No one knows who wrote them. No one is sure of their age.

Many cultures have marked their graves with commonplace sentiments. The best of the Greek epitaphs are different. Small vivid time capsules, they convey their brief testaments with surprising directness, in voices that frequently possess a modern ring. Many, perhaps most, Greek epitaphs are lost. Those that survive range widely across Greek society. Even in this slim selection, we meet soldiers, sailors, generals, admirals, philosophers, poets, priests, playwrights, paupers, fishermen, farmers, physicians, merchants, elders, infants, teachers, musicians, astronomers, tyrants, virgins, misers, undertakers, drunks, tycoons, crones, slaves, actors, dolphins, horses, insects, and farm animals, as well as people of no clear rank or occupation. Reading good Greek epitaphs, we learn a little something of Greek life. They show us, not merely how people died, but how they lived and what they cared about. And they accomplish this with an intimacy rare in Greek literature. They are vivid, not morbid.

Despite their size, Greek epitaphs by definition address eternal questions. What is a good death? What is tragic loss? What can be said of a loved one? What may be said of a stranger? Such range in so few words is extraordinary. One of the oldest samples, carved on a stone depicting a horse and rider (perhaps about to be thrown), memorializes a young man's exuberance while expressing the circularity of physical existence:

> After many high times with friends my age,
> I am back in the earth I sprang from:
> Aristocles. Menon's son. From Piraeus.

The sentiments expressed in the better Greek epitaphs are down to earth and genuine, only rarely arch or overly clever. By their emotional directness, they often achieve the clear simplicity of fine writing. When read in numbers, they compose a frank, human frieze depicting a world lost in time, yet familiar.

Though produced to honor the dead, Greek epitaphs may be arrestingly candid. When cast in the first person, the deceased seem to speak for themselves. Some are wryly funny—like the one for the comic actor Philistion (page 7), who played dying men on stage, "but never quite like this." Others are less pointedly ironic. The words of the suicide on page 11, for instance, are so understated that a reader may have to scan them twice to grasp their meaning—that the smile he wears in death is not an expression of good humor but a result of the muscle-constricting poison he chose to swallow.

Greek epitaphs deploy a rich variety of tones—stately, frank, comforting, heartfelt, heroic, ironic, lamenting, proud. In those that are actual tombstone verses, the voice of a family or third party may lurk in the background. On page 9, the young girl speaking in the first-person makes a flat statement: "*I will be known as a virgin for all time.*" The disappointment expressed is really her parents'—that she died childless. Their lament, free of false comfort, conveys an honest solace of its own. Or, take the bleak remarks of the man from Tarsus on page 8, who never married and wishes his father hadn't married either. Were these lines approved by the deceased before his death, or did someone compose them later? A person who knew him? A professional epigrammatist in the pay of a disgruntled neighbor? Spoken in first-person, the lines sum up a state of mind that readers in any age may recognize.

In Greek literature's infancy, centuries before the invention of scrolls and libraries, anonymous tombstone epitaphs offered passersby some of the first individual reading experiences in Western history. Utilitarian in purpose, their deeper inspiration springs from the urge to commemorate individuals and render them indelible, whether a local hero or a loved one.

Anonymous

I, the actor, Philistion
Soothed men's pain with comedy and laughter.
A man of parts, I often died
But never quite like this.

Ὁ τὸν πολυστένακτον ἀνθρώπων βίον
   γέλωτι κεράσας Νικαεὺς Φιλιστίων
ἐνταῦθα κεῖμαι, λείψανον παντὸς βίου,
   πολλάκις ἀποθανών, ὧδε δ' οὐδεπώποτε.

Anonymous

My name is Dionysius of Tarsus.
I was sixty when I died. I never married.
I wish my father hadn't married either.

Ἑξηκοντούτης Διονύσιος ἐνθάδε κεῖμαι,
Ταρσεύς, μὴ γήμας· αἴθε δὲ μηδ' ὁ πατήρ.

Anonymous

Phrasikleia's headstone says:
I will be called a virgin for all time.
This title I won from the gods
Instead of marriage.
–*Fashioned by* Aristion of Paros

Σῆμα Φρασικλείας· κούρη κεκλήσομαι αἰεί
ἀντί γάμου παρὰ θεῶν τοῦτο λαχοῦσ' ὄνομα.
Ἀριστίων Πάρι[ος μ' ἐπ]ό[η]σε.

Lines on a Pillar Depicting Amphareté Holding Her Grandchild

I hold my daughter's young one lovingly,
The one I held on my knee while we were living,
Back in the days when we blinked at the bright
sun–
The one I still hold here, though we have vanished.

Τέκνον ἐμῆς θυγατρός τόδ' ἔχω φίλον, ὅμπερ ὅτ' αὐγάς
ὄμμασιν ἠελίο ζῶντες ἐδερκόμεθα,
ἔχον ἐμοῖς γόνασιν καὶ νῦν φθίμενον φθιμένη 'χω.

Anonymous

I, unhappy Sophocles,
Entered Death's house grinning
Because I swallowed Sardinian celery
(A poison that contracts the lips).
And so I died, and others otherwise,
But all of us somehow or other.

Ἐνθάδ' ἐγὼ Σοφοκλῆς στυγερὸν δόμον Ἄϊδος ἔσβην
κάμμορος, εἴδατι Σαρδῴῳ σελίνοιο γελάσκων.
ὣς μὲν ἐγών, ἕτεροι δ' ἄλλως· πάντες δέ τε πάντως.

Anonymous

The way to the underworld is straight,
Whether one starts from Athens or the Nile.
Don't worry about dying far from home.
A fair breeze blows from every quarter
Right to the land of the dead.

Εἰς ἀΐδην ἰθεῖα κατήλυσις, εἴτ᾽ ἀπ᾽ Ἀθηνῶν
  στείχοις, εἴτε νέκυς νίσεαι ἐκ Μερόης.
μὴ σέ γ᾽ ἀνιάτω πάτρης ἀποτῆλε θανόντα·
  πάντοθεν εἷς ὁ φέρων εἰς ἀΐδην ἄνεμος.

Anonymous

I am dead, yet I await you.
You will wait for someone else.
In the land of the dead
A single death waits for everybody.

Κάτθανον, ἀλλὰ μένω σε· μενεῖς δέ τε καὶ σύ
τιν' ἄλλον·
πάντας ὁμῶς θνητοὺς εἷς Ἀΐδης δέχεται.

Anonymous

If good people survive once life is over,
Living on as speech in the mouths of men,
Then you, Andreas, thrive and are not dead.
A divine place with the sacred deathless ones
Awaits you, now that your work is done.

Εἰ γένος εὐσεβέων ζώει μετὰ τέρμα βίοιο,
ναιετάον κατὰ θεσμὸν ἀνὰ στόμα φωτὸς ἑκάστου,
Ἀνδρέα, σὺ ζώεις, οὐ κάτθανες· ἀλλά σε χῶρος
ἄμβροτος ἀθανάτων ἁγίων ὑπέδεκτο καμόντα.

Anonymous

Three times I reigned in Athens.
Three times the clan of Erechtheus ran me out.
Each time they called me back again:

Peisistratus, the great adviser,
Who brought together Homer's works
Only sung till then in bits and pieces.

(For Homer, worth his weight in gold,
Was in some ways one of us.
His birthplace, Smyrna, we made a colony.)

Τρίς με τυραννήσαντα τοσαυτάκις ἐξεδίωξεν
δῆμος Ἐρεχθῆος, καὶ τρὶς ἐπηγάγετο,
τὸν μέγαν ἐν βουλῇ Πεισίστρατον, ὃς τὸν Ὅμηρον
ἤθροισα, σποράδην τὸ πρὶν ἀειδόμενον·
ἡμέτερος γὰρ κεῖνος ὁ χρύσεος ἦν πολιήτης,
εἴπερ Ἀθηναῖοι Σμύρναν ἀπῳκίσαμεν.

Anonymous Inscription, Athens, Sixth Century BCE

Whether you come from here or not,
Pity Tettichos as you pass–

A man of valor cut down in action,
Robbed of youth on the battlefield.

Mourn him a minute.
Then get busy doing something good.

[Εἴτ' ἀστό]ς τις ἀνὴρ εἴτε ξένος ἄλ(λ)οθεν ἐλθὼν
Τέτ(τ)ιχον οἰκτίρας ἄνδρ' ἀγαθὸν παρίτω
ἐν πολέμωι φθίμενον, νεαρὰν ἥβην ὀλέσαντα·
ταῦτ' ἀποδυράμενοι νεῖσθε ἐπὶ πρᾶγμ' ἀγαθόν.

Anonymous

After many high times with friends my age,
I am back in the earth I sprang from:
Aristocles. Menon's son. From Piraeus.

Πολλὰ μεθ' ἡλικίας ὁμοήλικος ἡδέα παίσας,
  ἐκ γαίας βλαστὼν γαῖα πάλιν γέγονα·
εἰμὶ δὲ Ἀριστοκλῆς Πειραιεύς, παῖς δὲ Μένωνος.

Epitaph on the Grave of Sardanapallus

What I ate and drank I take with me,
Along with the delights I learned from lovers,
But the blessing of all my possessions
I leave behind.

Τόσσ' ἔχω ὅσσ' ἔφαγον καὶ ἔπιον, καὶ μετ' ἐρώτων
τέρπν' ἐδάην· τὰ δὲ πολλὰ καὶ ὄλβια πάντα
λέλειπται.

Anonymous

A modest tomb. Yet see how the fame
Of thoughtful Thales reaches to the sky!

Ἦ ὀλίγον τόδε σᾶμα, τὸ δὲ κλέος οὐρανόμηκες
τοῦ πολυφροντίστου τοῦτο Θάλητος ὅρη.

II

Late Archaic and Classical Periods, 600–350 BCE

A small group of well-known epigrams have traditionally been assigned to the first Greek lyric poets and to several later literary luminaries. According to this tradition, early in the sixth century canonical innovators of the Greek lyric, like Sappho and Anacreon, crafted masterful elegiac couplets and tombstone verse. Similar contributions to the genre followed, by the legendary commemorative poet Simonides (556–468 BCE), the early dramatist Aeschylus (525–456 BCE), and the philosopher Plato (427–348 BCE), among others. Today, modern scholars persuasively argue that most if not all of these venerable entries are literary forgeries composed by poets of a later age.

Complete surviving poems by Sappho and Anacreon are all but nonexistent. Among their remaining fragments no epigrams appear – only those "preserved" in the much later Greek Anthology. The purpose of attributing epitaphs and epigrams to these two early giants of lyric poetry seems to have been to confer respect by association on poets and poems written centuries later in the Hellenistic period.

A few of the many epitaphs ascribed to Simonides may rest on firmer ground. Simonides flourished in the early fifth century, when Greece's small city-states were first invaded by mammoth Persia and when courage against great odds was especially prized. Unsigned epitaphs, set on pillars, were commissioned at this time to memorialize Greek heroes who had fallen in battle. In particular, three poems in the Anthology which are assigned to Simonides are also quoted by a near-contemporary, the historian Herodotus, in his description of the battle at Thermopylae (see pages 31, 32, and 33). While this may establish the age of the verses, we have only the assertion of an often unreliable author that one of them was composed by Simonides.

The playwright Aeschylus lived in the same period. He fought the Persians at Marathon (490 BCE) and elsewhere. The play he wrote later concerning their defeat is the oldest complete Greek drama we possess. In an epitaph (page 40) ascribed to him in the Anthology, this highly honored Athenian dramatist asks only to be remembered as a soldier. Though certainly not by Aeschylus, the poem underscores the primacy of service to one's city that defined Athenian character in his time.

By contrast, epitaphs under the names of lesser fifth-century poets like Cleoboulus and Isidorus seem correctly attributed. Anonymous poets wrote fine epitaphs in this period, too. At the battle of Salamis, an unknown author set in stone a poignant fraternal testament to a defeated leader:

To our towering friendship
I've raised this little stone.
Sabinus, I will look for you forever . . .

The epigrams attributed to Plato a few decades later reflect a popular belief that, before he turned to philosophy, this masterful practitioner of Greek prose tried his hand at verse. Certainly several of the epitaphs ascribed to him are memorable. Shelley singled out one of them as the best short poem of its kind. Nonetheless, Plato is almost certainly not the author of these pieces.

By now, experts have reassigned most of the poems in the following section to anonymous poets of the third century BCE, who wrote them to manufacture a venerable tradition, either for the genre itself or for the historical figures they memorialize. Provenance aside, their artful language and emotional clarity help rank some of them among the best epitaphs in Greek. It is a tribute to their nameless makers that for centuries native Greek readers, including expert anthologists, accepted the famous names attached to them as real.

Sappho

This dust is Timas, struck down before she could
  wed.
Persephone's dark bridal hall received her.
When she died, her girlfriends
All sharpened blades and sheared their gorgeous
  hair.

Τιμάδος ἅδε κόνις, τὰν δὴ πρὸ γάμοιο θανοῦσαν
  δέξατο Φερσεφόνας κυάνεος θάλαμος,
ἆς καὶ ἀποφθιμένας πᾶσαι νεοθᾶγι σιδάρῳ
  ἄλικες ἱμερτὰν κρατὸς ἔθεντο κόμαν.

Cleoboulos

I am a girl made of bronze resting on Midas's grave.
As long as water runs and tall trees spread,
I'll stand on this tomb where the tears keep flowing,
To tell all those who pass: Midas lies here.

Χαλκῆ παρθένος εἰμί, Μίδα δ' ἐπὶ σήματι κεῖμαι.
ἔστ' ἂν ὕδωρ τε νάῃ, καὶ δένδρεα μακρὰ τεθήλῃ,
αὐτοῦ τῇδε μένουσα πολυκλαύτῳ ἐπὶ τύμβῳ,
ἀγγελέω παριοῦσι, Μίδας ὅτι τῇδε τέθαπται.

Anacreon

Courageous Timocritus, this is his grave.
War spares the coward, not the brave.

Καρτερὸς ἐν πολέμοις Τιμόκριτος, οὗ τόδε σᾶμα·
Ἄρης δ᾽ οὐκ ἀγαθῶν φείδεται, ἀλλὰ κακῶν.

Anacreon

While the fearsome warrior Agathon
Who died fighting for Abdera
Lay stretched on a funeral pyre
The whole town shouted out his praise,

For the bloodthirsty war god Ares
Who stripped away his armor
Dragged down no boy like him
In the swirling eddy of that awful fight.

Ἀβδήρων προθανόντα τὸν αἰνοβίην Ἀγάθωνα
πᾶσ' ἐπὶ πυρκαΐῆς ἥδ' ἐβόησε πόλις.
οὔ τινα γὰρ τοιόνδε νέων ὁ φιλαίματος Ἄρης
ἠνάρισεν στυγερῆς ἐν στροφάλιγγι μάχης.

Simonides

This is the tomb of Megistias,
Slain by the Medes at Thermopylae.
Famous prophet, he knew what was coming.
Still, he wouldn't leave the Spartan side.

Μνῆμα τόδε κλεινοῖο Μεγιστίου, ὅν ποτε Μῆδοι
  Σπερχειὸν ποταμὸν κτεῖναν ἀμειψάμενοι,
μάντιος, ὃς τότε κῆρας ἐπερχομένας σάφα εἰδὼς
  οὐκ ἔτλη Σπάρτης ἡγεμόνας προλιπεῖν.

Simonides

Three million [Persians] fought here once
With four thousand men from the Peloponnese.

Μυριάσιν ποτὲ τῇδε τριηκοσίαις ἐμάχοντο
ἐκ Πελοποννάσου χιλιάδες τέτορες.

Simonides

Stranger, take the news back to the Spartans
That we lie here, who followed their commands.

Ὦ ξεῖν', ἄγγειλον Λακεδαιμονίοις ὅτι τῇδε
κείμεθα, τοῖς κείνων ῥήμασι πειθόμενοι.

Simonides

After drinking a lot, eating a lot
And speaking badly of everyone,
Here I lie, Timocreon of Rhodes.

Πολλὰ πιὼν καὶ πολλὰ φαγών, καὶ πολλὰ κάκ' εἰπὼν
ἀνθρώπους, κεῖμαι Τιμοκρέων Ῥόδιος.

Simonides

No grand tomb fit for Croesus do you see,
But a small workman's grave: enough for me.

Ἄνθρωπ', οὐ Κροίσου λεύσσεις τάφον, ἀλλὰ γὰρ
ἀνδρὸς
χερνήτεω μικρὸς τύμβος, ἐμοὶ δ' ἱκανός.

Simonides

I Brotachus of Crete now lie unmade,
Who came here not to die but just for trade.

Κρὴς γενεὰν Βρόταχος Γορτύνιος ἐνθάδε κεῖμαι,
οὐ κατὰ τοῦτ᾽ ἐλθών, ἀλλὰ κατ᾽ ἐμπορίην.

Isidorus of Aegae

This rise in the ground is someone's grave.
Back off the oxen, raise the plough:
You're stirring up human ashes.
Don't sow grain on land like this. Shed tears!

Τὸ χῶμα τύμβος ἐστίν· ἀλλὰ τὼ βόε
 ἐπίσχες οὗτος, τὰν ὕνιν τ' ἀνάσπασον·
κινεῖς σποδὸν γάρ. ἐς δὲ τοιαύταν κόνιν
 μὴ σπέρμα πυρῶν, ἀλλὰ χεῦε δάκρυα.

Isidorus of Aegae

I am Eteocles, bred to farm,
Then lured away by trade and the sea's promise
To be a merchant.
Skimming along the Tyrrhenian waves,
My ship went down in a sudden squall.
Now I know: The wind that swells a sail
Is not the breeze that sweeps the threshing floor.

Ἔκ με γεωμορίης Ἐτεοκλέα πόντιος ἐλπὶς
  εἵλκυσεν, ὀθνείης ἔμπορον ἐργασίης·
νῶτα δὲ Τυρσηνῆς ἐπάτευν ἁλός· ἀλλ' ἅμα νηῒ
  πρηνιχθεὶς κείνης ὕδασιν ἐγκατέδυν,
ἀθρόον ἐμβρίσαντος ἀήματος. οὐκ ἄρ' ἀλωὰς
  αὐτὸς ἐπιπνείει κεὶς ὀθόνας ἄνεμος.

Anonymous Inscription at the Battle of Salamis, 480 BCE

To our towering friendship
I've raised this little stone.
Sabinus, I will look for you forever.
If things turn out as people say
And you join the dead,
To drink from the river
That helps men forget,
Please don't drink the drop
That makes you forget me.

Τοῦτό τοι ἡμετέρης μνημήϊον, ἐσθλὲ Σαβῖνε,
ἡ λίθος ἡ μικρή, τῆς μεγάλης φιλίης.
αἰεὶ ζητήσω σε· σὺ δ', εἰ θέμις, ἐν φθιμένοισι
τοῦ Λήθης ἐπ' ἐμοὶ μή τι πίῃς ὕδατος.

Aeschylus

This monument holds Aeschylus,
Euphorion's son, from Athens.

He lies here at Gela in Sicily
Among the fields of wheat.

Yet the far-off forests of Marathon
Bear witness to his bravery,

And the long-haired Persian he battled there
Could tell you of his strength.

Αἰσχύλον Εὐφορίωνος Ἀθηναῖον τόδε κεύθει
  μνῆμα καταφθίμενον πυροφόροιο Γέλας.
ἀλκὴν δ' εὐδόκιμον Μαραθώνιον ἄλσος ἂν εἴποι
  καὶ βαθυχαιτήεις Μῆδος ἐπιστάμενος.

Plato

I am the grave of a shipwrecked man.
Over there lies the tomb of a farmer.
On sea and land alike
Death lies in wait.

Ναυηγοῦ τάφος εἰμί ·ὁ δ' ἀντίον ἐστὶ γεωργοῦ·
ὡς ἁλὶ καὶ γαίῃ ξυνὸς ὕπεστ' Ἀΐδης.

Plato

Here you see a shipwrecked man.
The ocean, which showed some pity,
Didn't dare strip me of my last rag.

It took a man with brazen hands to do that,
Weighing down his soul for next to nothing.

Let him put it on then.
Let him take it to Hell with him.
Let Minos catch him wearing my old jacket.

Ναυηγόν με δέδορκας. ὃν οἰκτείρασα θάλασσα
  γυμνῶσαι πυμάτου φάρεος ᾐδέσατο,
ἄνθρωπος παλάμῃσιν ἀταρβήτοις μ' ἀπέδυσε,
  τόσσον ἄγος τόσσου κέρδεος ἀράμενος.
κεῖνο καὶ ἐνδύσαιτο, καὶ εἰς Ἀΐδαο φέροιτο,
  καί μιν ἴδοι Μίνως τοὐμὸν ἔχοντα ῥάκος.

Plato:
For Aster

Now you lie face up beneath the stars,
My Star.

If only I were the night sky,
I would gaze on you with many eyes.

Ἀστέρας εἰσαθρεῖς ἀστὴρ ἐμός. εἴθε γενοίμην
Οὐρανός, ὡς πολλοῖς ὄμμασιν εἰς σὲ βλέπω.

III

Hellenistic Period

Age of Alexander, c. 323–100 BCE

Of the many surviving tombstone verses composed before the late fourth century BCE, a great majority are serviceable, sentimental, nothing special. Beginning early in the third century, however, the epigram, and so the epitaph, were rapidly refined into a sophisticated literary form capable of depicting contemporary Alexandrian life in all its physical, social, and emotional complexity.

Three poets led this transformation: Leonidas of Tarentum, Anyte of Tegea, and Nossis of Locri. Working independently, this trio and their many contemporaries wrenched the epigram away from its time-honored topics of military prowess, elite social values, and male dominion. They personalized its voice, diversified its rhetorical style, and expanded its social range.

Significantly, two of these innovators, Anyte and Nossis, were women. Their distance from the centers of power is telling. Leonidas and Nossis lived in the rural south of Italy, within a hundred miles of each other, while Anyte wrote from a remote part of the Peloponnese. Together, these provincials relocated the epigram in pastoral settings, feminine values, and a celebration of life among common, nonheroic Greeks. Both women were aristocrats. Leonidas also may have been well born. They wrote with sophistication, yet their shared vision is plainly democratic.

Leonidas was the widest ranging and most prolific epigrammatist of the period. His one hundred surviving poems stand at the opposite end of a spectrum from the noble simplicity of Simonides. His generous epitaphs for fishermen, farmers, and ascetics form a representative album of lower-class Greeks, many of whom led hard lives near the bottom of the social ladder. Although they have the feel of true memorials, his epitaphs are largely literary inventions. Like the work of the early-twentieth-century American poet Edgar Lee Masters in his *Spoon River Anthology*, the epigrams of Leonidas may be read as a literary project that collectively portrays the common man.

Nossis, Leonidas's neighbor, quietly glorified the social lives of contemporary women. Her choice of themes, including lesbian allusions harking back to Sappho, threw open the doors of the male-dominated epigram. Greeks prized her for her lyric sweetness (*melopoiea*). Unfortunately, only two epitaphs by Nossis survive. One is a message across the centuries to Sappho (page 72). The other (page 73) celebrates the work of a local playwright, Rhinthon, whose satires of Classical tragedy she admired.

Anyte wrote like a Spartan, chastely, often on rural themes. With twenty-five entries to her name in the Greek Anthology, we have more complete poems by

Anyte than by any other woman of ancient Greece. A number of these are epitaphs, some for women and some for domestic animals, including dogs, cats, roosters, and even a child's pet cricket and cicada. As with Nossis, Anyte's works made important departures from conventional subject matter. Like Sappho, she harmonized strong feelings with a delicate verbal music.

Callimachus, her near contemporary, may be the most polished epigrammatist of this or any period. A Libyan from Cyrene, resident in Egypt, he was the complete Hellenic man of letters–scholar, sophisticate, courtier and, not incidentally, closely associated with the ancient world's most respected library. The American poet Kenneth Rexroth called him an Alexandrian Voltaire. Callimachus wrote in many forms, but the wit and succinctness of the epigram suited him perfectly. Brevity and compression were his ideals–"Big book, bad book" he quipped, dismissing the epic. In the epitaph on page 77, he associates the reticence of a laconic Cretan with his own passion for economy. Callimachus's many epitaphs display a genius for blending character and aesthetics, distilling to luminous essentials the lives of men and women of every class.

These poets of the Hellenistic Period expressed the societal sea-change of their times. In the previous, Classical period of Periclean Athens (circa 495–429 BCE), a community-minded dedication to one's city-state frequently muted expressions of personal emotion, while a passion for logic and metaphysics overshadowed verse. (The quintessential Athenian philosopher, Plato, banished poets from his imaginary utopia.) In the next century, however, with the decline of mainland city-states and the breathtaking spread of Greek culture throughout Asia, the Nile Valley, and the Mediterranean, this age of local, public values receded. In its place a cosmopolitan period of more diverse concerns began that included fresh interest in the personal themes of family life and intimacy. Something like the Romantic Age emerged, in which pastoral beauty was elevated and the lyric and epigram entered a heyday. In philosophy, the schools of Stoicism, Skepticism, and Epicureanism emerged, expressing distinct versions of the individualist's creed.

Recent scholarship suggests that Anyte may have composed and circulated the first personal collection of epigrams in Greek. If so, she initiated a trend that moved the epigram from the margins of an inscriptional tradition to a central place in written literature. Today, we take for granted the slim collection of poetry by one author. In the third century BCE this was still an emerging form, one that encouraged the poet to shape a personal voice while providing the reader a place to find and hear it. The individual scrolls of epigrams by Leonidas, Nossis, Anyte, and Callimachus may just constitute the first contemporary poetry books in Western literature.

Leonidas of Tarentum

Old Theris lived by his fish traps.
He spent more time at sea than any gull.
A seine net pirate, a cave diver
He probed the rocks for eel and crab
And never sailed on show boats.
Despite so many years at sea
He didn't drown in an autumn squall
Or see his life cut short by a storm.
He died at home in a reed hut,
Going out like a lamp
Because he was ancient.
No wife or son set up this tomb
But his friends in the divers' union.

Θῆριν τὸν τριγέροντα, τὸν εὐάγρων ἀπὸ κύρτων
ζῶντα, τὸν αἰθυίης πλείονα νηξάμενον,
ἰχθυσιληϊστῆρα, σαγηνέα, χηραμοδύτην,
οὐχὶ πολυσκάλμου πλώτορα ναυτιλίης,
ἔμπης οὔτ' Ἀρκτοῦρος ἀπώλεσεν, οὔτε καταιγὶς
ἤλασε τὰς πολλὰς τῶν ἐτέων δεκάδας·
ἀλλ' ἔθαν' ἐν καλύβῃ σχοινίτιδι, λύχνος ὁποῖα,
τῷ μακρῷ σβεσθεὶς ἐν χρόνῳ αὐτόματος.
σῆμα δὲ τοῦτ' οὐ παῖδες ἐφήρμοσαν, οὐδ' ὁμόλεκτρος,
ἀλλὰ συνεργατίνης ἰχθυβόλων θίασος.

Leonidas of Tarentum

Don't trust too much in the length or draft of
your vessel.
One gust is all it takes to sink a ship,

As when a single blast destroyed Promachus.
One tall wave sent him to the bottom.

Still, fate was not entirely unkind.
A rough sea pitched his body on the beach.

There he received a funeral in his homeland,
A tomb and burial by his countrymen.

Μήτε μακρῇ θαρσέων ναυτίλλεο μήτε βαθείῃ
νηΐ· κρατεῖ παντὸς δούρατος εἷς ἄνεμος.
ὤλεσε καὶ Πρόμαχον πνοιὴ μία, κῦμα δ' ἓν αὔτως
ἀθρόον ἐς κοίλην ἐστυφέλιξεν ἅλα.
οὐ μήν οἱ δαίμων πάντη κακός· ἀλλ' ἐνὶ γαίῃ
πατρίδι καὶ τύμβου καὶ κτερέων ἔλαχεν
κηδεμόνων ἐν χερσίν, ἐπεὶ τρηχεῖα θάλασσα
νεκρὸν πεπταμένους θῆκεν ἐπ' αἰγιαλούς.

Leonidas of Tarentum

This shed where Kleito lived is cramped,
His seed patch just a tiny strip,
His vineyard scant, his woodland scrubby.
Yet Kleito lasted eighty years here.

Τοῦτ' [ὀλίγον] Κλείτωνος ἐπαύλιον, ἥ τ' ὀλιγῶλαξ
  σπείρεσθαι, λιτός θ' ὁ σχεδὸν ἀμπελεών,
τοῦτό τε †ῥωπεῖον ὀλιγόξυλον· ἀλλ' ἐπὶ τούτοις
  Κλείτων ὀγδώκοντ' ἐξεπέρησ' ἔτεα.

Leonidas of Tarentum

I am a stone on top of Kretho,
Declaring the man's name.
Kretho is the ashes underneath me.

He once matched Gyges in his wealth,
He once owned countless herds,
He once–but why repeat things?
He was everybody's envy.

What a small patch of that great estate
Is his.

Αὕτα ἐπὶ Κρήθωνος ἐγὼ λίθος, οὔνομα κείνου
δηλοῦσα· Κρήθων δ᾽ ἐν χθονίοις σποδιά.
ὁ πρὶν καὶ Γύγῃ παρισεύμενος ὄλβον, ὁ τὸ πρὶν
βουπάμων, ὁ πρὶν πλούσιος αἰπολίοις,
ὁ πρίν—τί πλείω μυθεῦμαι; ὁ πᾶσι μακαρτός,
φεῦ, γαίης ὅσσης ὅσσον ἔχει μόριον.

Leonidas of Tarentum

Like a vine on a stake I lean on this stick.
When death calls out, I won't play deaf.
What pleasure can sunbathing hold for me
For three or four more summers?

Speaking quiet words like these,
Ancient Gorgos cast off life, moving on
To the place of the great majority.

"Ἄμπελος ὥς ἤδη κάμακι στηρίζομαι αὐτῷ
σκηπανίῳ· καλέει μ' εἰς ἀΐδην θάνατος.
δυσκώφει μὴ Γόργε· τί τοι χαριέστερον, ἢ τρεῖς
ἢ πίσυρας ποίας θάλψαι ὑπ' ἠελίῳ;"
ὧδ' εἴπας οὐ κόμπῳ, ἀπὸ ζωὴν ὁ παλαιὸς
ὤσατο, κὴς πλεόνων ἦλθε μετοικεσίην.

Leonidas of Tarentum

A light dusting of earth is fine for me.
Let the lavish, high-priced stone
Crush some other man at rest–
A hard burden for the dead to bear.

Now that I've died,
How should being noticed matter
To Alcander, son of Calliteles?

Ἀρκεῖ μοι γαίης μικρὴ κόνις· ἡ δὲ περισσὴ
ἄλλον ἐπιθλίβοι πλούσια κεκλιμένον
στήλη, τὸ σκληρὸν νεκρῶν βάρος· ἔι με θανόντα
γνώσοντ', Ἀλκάνδρῳ τοῦτο τί Καλλιτέλευς;

Leonidas of Tarentum

A headlong savage southeastern squall
And night and the waves Orion whips up
When it sets in dark November
Were my downfall.

I, Callaiskhros, slipped out of life
Sailing the deep-sea shelf off Libya.
Now I am lost, swirled here and there,
A miserable prey to the fishes.

The stone on my grave claims
Callaiskhros lies here.
What a liar.

Εὔρου με τρηχεῖα καὶ αἰπήεσσα καταιγίς,
  καὶ νύξ, καὶ δνοφερῆς κύματα πανδυσίης
ἔβλαψ' Ὠρίωνος· ἀπώλισθον δὲ βίοιο
  Κάλλαισχρος, Λιβυκοῦ μέσσα θέων πελάγευς.
κἀγὼ μὲν πόντῳ δινεύμενος, ἰχθύσι κῦρμα,
  οἴχημαι· ψεύστης δ' οὗτος ἔπεστι λίθος.

Leonidas of Tarentum

Sea in an uproar,
When I met my end
Why didn't you spit me out
Far from this beach,

So that even shrouded in hellish fog
Phyleus, son of Amphimenes,
Would not have to lie
Next to you forever.

Τετρηχυῖα θάλασσα, τί μ' οὐκ οἰζυρὰ παθόντα
τηλόσ' ἀπὸ ψιλῆς ἔπτυσας ἠϊόνος;
ὡς σεῦ μηδ' Ἀΐδαο κακὴν ἐπιειμένος ἀχλὺν
Φυλεὺς Ἀμφιμένευς ἆσσον ἐγειτόνεον.

Leonidas of Tarentum

A wallet, a goatskin hard as rock,
A walking stick, a grimy flask,
A purse with nothing in it and
This hat to shade his Cynic's head
Were all Sochares had. The day he died,
Starvation hung them in the bushes for him.

Πήρην, κἀδέψητον ἀπεσκληρυμμένον αἰγὸς
  στέρφος, καὶ βάκτρον τοῦτό γ' ὁδοιπορικόν,
κώλπαν ἀστλέγγιστον, ἀχάλκωτόν τε κυνοῦχον,
  καὶ πῖλον κεφαλᾶς οὐχ ὁσίας σκέπανον·
ταῦτα καταφθιμένοιο μυρικίνεον περὶ θάμνον
  σκῦλ' ἀπὸ Σωχάρεος Λιμὸς ἀνεκρέμασεν.

Leonidas of Tarentum

Step softly past this poet's grave.
Don't stir the freshly burrowed wasp asleep here.
Hipponax tormented his own parents.
Be careful.
Forged in fire, his words still sting,
Even in Hades.

'Ατρέμα τὸν τύμβον παραμείβετε, μὴ τὸν ἐν ὕπνῳ
πικρὸν ἐγείρητε σφῆκ' ἀναπαυόμενον.
ἄρτι γὰρ Ἱππώνακτος ὁ καὶ τοκέωνε βαΰξας
ἄρτι κεκοίμηται θυμὸς ἐν ἡσυχίῃ.
ἀλλὰ προμηθήσασθε· τὰ γὰρ πεπυρωμένα κείνου
ῥήματα πημαίνειν οἶδε καὶ εἰν Ἀΐδῃ.

Leonidas of Tarentum

Passing here
Recall Eubulus,
who never drank a drop.

Then, let's drink.
All people share one port—
The underworld.

Μέμνησθ' Εὐβούλοιο σαόφρονος, ὦ παριόντες.
πίνωμεν· κοινὸς πᾶσι λιμὴν Ἀΐδης.

Leonidas of Tarentum

Maronis the wino, who drained dry every glass,
Lies in this tomb topped by an Attic cup.

Deep in the bowels of Earth she sheds a tear,
Not for the husband and children

She drank out of house and home, but rather
For the cup—seeing it's empty.

Μαρωνὶς ἡ φίλοινος, ἡ πίθων σποδός,
ἐνταῦθα κεῖται γρῆϋς, ἧς ὑπὲρ τάφου
γνωστὸν πρόκειται πᾶσιν Ἀττικὴ κύλιξ.
στένει δὲ καὶ γᾶς νέρθεν, οὐχ ὑπὲρ τέκνων,
οὐδ' ἀνδρός, οὕς λέλοιπεν ἐνδεεῖς βίου·
ἓν δ' ἀντὶ πάντων, οὕνεχ' ἡ κύλιξ κενή.

Posidippus

Three-year-old Archianax, playing near a well,
Was drawn down by his own silent reflection.

His mother, afraid he had no breath left,
Hauled him back up wringing wet. He had a
little.

He didn't taint the nymphs' deep home.
He dozed off in her lap. He's sleeping still.

Τὸν τριετῆ παίζοντα περὶ φρέαρ Ἀρχιάνακτα
εἴδωλον μορφᾶς κωφὸν ἐπεσπάσατο·
ἐκ δ' ὕδατος τὸν παῖδα διάβροχον ἥρπασε μάτηρ
σκεπτομένα ζωᾶς εἴ τινα μοῖραν ἔχει·
Νύμφας δ'οὐκ ἐμίηνεν ὁ νήπιος, ἀλλ' ἐπὶ γούνων
ματρὸς κοιμαθεὶς τὸν βαθὺν ὕπνον ἔχει.

Anyte

All his life this man was a slave named Prince.
Dead, he is the equal of King Darius.

Μάνης οὗτος ἀνὴρ ἦν ζῶν ποτέ· νῦν δὲ τεθνηκὼς
ἶσον Δαρείῳ τῷ μεγάλῳ δύναται.

Anyte:
To a Rooster

You will never waken me again
Rising early, flapping those quick wings.

While you dozed, a trespasser stole in
Ripping out your throat with lightning claws.

Οὐκέτι μ’ ὡς τὸ πάρος πυκιναῖς πτερύγεσσιν
    ἐρέσσων
  ὄρσεις ἐξ εὐνῆς ὄρθριος ἐγρόμενος·
ἦ γάρ σ’ ὑπνώοντα σίνις λαθρηδὸν ἐπελθὼν
  ἔκτεινεν λαιμῷ ῥίμφα καθεὶς ὄνυχα.

Anyte

For the locust caught in a wheat field
With its nightingale voice,
And for the cicada she found clinging to a tree
Myra has set up a single tomb,
Shedding the tear of a young girl,
For implacable death has carried off her
  playmates.

Ἀκρίδι τᾷ κατ' ἄρουραν ἀηδόνι, καὶ δρυοκοίτᾳ
  τέττιγι ξυνὸν τύμβον ἔτευξε Μυρώ,
παρθένιον στάξασα κόρα δάκρυ· δισσὰ γὰρ αὐτᾶς
  παίγνι' ὁ δυσπειθὴς ᾤχετ' ἔχων Ἀΐδας.

Anyte:
A Dolphin

I will never again delight in buoyant seas,
Rocketing up from the depths, neck thrust out
  of the water,

Nor circle an oarlocked ship, long lips grinning,
Pleased to find my own bust carved on the bow.

Dark waters dashed me to the land.
I lie here on a narrow strip of sand.

Οὐκέτι δὴ πλωτοῖσιν ἀγαλλόμενος πελάγεσσιν
  αὐχέν' ἀναρρίψω βυσσόθεν ὀρνύμενος,
οὐδὲ περὶ †σκαλάμοισι νεὼς περικαλλέα χείλη
  ποιφύσσω, τᾀμᾷ τερπόμενος προτομᾷ·
ἀλλά με πορφυρέα πόντου νοτὶς ὦσ' ἐπὶ χέρσον,
  κεῖμαι δὲ †ῥαδινὰν τάνδε παρ' ἠϊόνα.

Anyte:
A Horse

Damis raised this stone for his staunch
Horse, after the war-god pierced its sorrel
Chest and black blood gushed through its thick
Hide, soaking the earth in its death-throes.

Μνᾶμα τόδε φθιμένου μενεδαΐου εἵσατο Δᾶμις
ἵππου, ἐπεὶ στέρνον τοῦδε δαφοινὸς Ἄρης
τύψε· μέλαν δέ οἱ αἷμα ταλαυρίνου διὰ χρωτὸς
ζέσσ', ἐπὶ δ' ἀργαλέᾳ βῶλον ἔδευσε φονᾷ.

Mnasalcas

Stranger, spread the news:
This tomb holds a mare named Seagull.
Fastest creature on dry land,
Her feet ran like the wind.

Racing cross-country,
She covered as much ground
As those sailing ships
The seabirds chase across the sound.

Αἰθυίας, ξένε, τόνδε ποδηνέμου ἔννεπε τύμβον,
τᾶς ποτ᾽ ἐλαφρότατον χέρσος ἔθρεψε γόνυ·
πολλάκι γὰρ νάεσσιν ἰσόδρομον ἄνυσε μᾶκος,
ὄρνις ὅπως δολιχὰν ἐκπονέουσα τρίβον.

Nossis of Locri

Stranger, if you sail to Lesbos,
Where gorgeous dancers
Once set Sappho,
The Graces' flower, on fire

Tell them: the land of Locri too
Bore one the Muses loved
Who was her equal.
My name is Nossis. *Go!*

Ὦ ξεῖν', εἰ τύ γε πλεῖς ποτὶ καλλίχορον Μυτιλάναν,
τὰν Σαπφὼ χαρίτων ἄνθος ἐναυσαμέναν,
εἰπεῖν, ὡς Μούσαισι φίλαν τήνᾳ τε Λοκρὶς γᾶ
τίκτεν ἴσαν ὅτι θ' οἱ τοὔνομα Νοσσίς· ἴθι.

Nossis of Locri

Laugh out loud as you pass here, Stranger.
Speak a word of kindness over me.
I'm Rhinthon of Syracuse,
One of the Muses' lesser songbirds.
Satirizing tragedies,
I earned a crown of laurel all my own.

Καὶ καπυρὸν γελάσας παραμείβεο, καὶ φίλον εἰπὼν
ῥῆμ' ἐπ' ἐμοί. Ῥίνθων ἔιμ' ὁ Συρακόσιος,
Μουσάων ὀλίγη τις ἀηδονίς· ἀλλὰ φλυάκων
ἐκ τραγικῶν ἴδιον κισσὸν ἐδρεψάμεθα.

Phalaecus

Avoid working at sea.
Take up the ox-drawn plow if you want a long
 life.
On land old age is possible.
At sea it's hard to find a grey-haired man.

Φεῦγε θαλάσσια ἔργα, βοῶν δ' ἐπιβάλλευ ἐχέτλῃ,
 εἴ τί τοι ἡδὺ μακρῆς πείρατ' ἰδεῖν βιοτῆς·
ἠπείρῳ γὰρ ἔνεστι μακρὸς βίος· εἰν ἁλὶ δ' οὔ πως
 εὐμαρὲς εἱς πολιὴν ἀνδρὸς ἰδεῖν κεφαλήν.

Callimachus

This tomb you are passing holds Callimachus.
He wrote good poems,
And timed his jokes at parties so
That everybody laughed.

Βαττιάδεω παρὰ σῆμα φέρεις πόδας, εὖ μὲν ἀοιδὴν
εἰδότος, εὖ δ' οἴνῳ καίρια συγγελάσαι.

Callimachus

Here sleeps Saon from Acanthus, Dicon's son.
Don't say good men are dead.

Τᾷδε Σάων ὁ Δίκωνος Ἀκάνθιος ἱερὸν ὕπνον
κοιμᾶται. θνάσκειν μὴ λέγε τοὺς ἀγαθούς.

Callimachus

This stranger was cut short. So is my song,
No lengthy oration: "Theris Aristaides, of
  Crete" –
To me that's long.

Σύντομος ἦν ὁ ξεῖνος· ὃ καὶ στίχος· οὐ μακρὰ λέξω·
  "Θῆρις Ἀρισταίου, Κρὴς" ἐπ' ἐμοὶ δόλιχος.

Callimachus

Here Phillip, a father, laid down his highest hope:
A twelve-year-old son, Nicoteles.

Δωδεκέτη τὸν παῖδα πατὴρ ἀπέθηκε Φίλιππος
ἐνθάδε, τὴν πολλὴν ἐλπίδα, Νικοτέλην.

Callimachus

"Farewell, Sun," young Cleombrotus cried
And leapt from a high wall straight down into
Hades,

Not because he had seen things that called for
suicide
But because he had read Plato's treatise on the
soul.

Εἴπας "ἥλιε, χαῖρε" Κλεόμβροτος ὡμβρακιώτης
ἥλατ' ἀφ' ὑψηλοῦ τείχεος εἰς ἀΐδαν,
ἄξιον οὐδὲν ἰδὼν θανάτου κακόν, ἀλλὰ Πλάτωνος
ἓν τὸ περὶ ψυχῆς γράμμ' ἀναλεξάμενος.

Callimachus

A brimming bowl of straight red wine
Knocked back twice without a pause
Has carried off Erasixenos, the binge drinker.

Τὸν βαθὺν οἰνοπότην Ἐρασίξενον ἡ δὶς ἐφεξῆς
ἀκρήτου προποθεῖσ᾽ ᾤχετ᾽ ἔχουσα κύλιξ.

Callimachus:
A Conversation

– *Is Charidas beneath this stone?*
STONE: If you mean the son of Arimmas the Libyan,
yes.
– *Charidas, what is down there?*
Great darkness.
– *Any way back up?*
All lies.
– *And Pluto?*
A myth.
– *Then we really perish!*
I'm just stating facts. If it's good news you're
after,
A large ox costs a dime in the land of the dead.

α. Ἦ ῥ' ὑπὸ σοὶ Χαρίδας ἀναπαύεται; β. Εἰ τὸν Ἀρίμμα
τοῦ Κυρηναίου παῖδα λέγεις, ὑπ' ἐμοί.
β. Ὦ Χαρίδα, τί τὰ νέρθε; γ. Πολὺς σκότος. α. Αἱ δ'
ἄνοδοι τί;
γ. Ψεῦδος. α. Ὁ δὲ Πλούτων; γ. Μῦθος. α. Ἀπωλόμεθα.
γ. Οὗτος ἐμὸς λόγος ὔμμιν ἀληθινός· εἰ δὲ τὸν ἡδὺν
βούλει, πελλαίου βοῦς μέγας εἰν ἀΐδῃ.

Callimachus

If you come to Hades
Looking for Timarchus,
To learn about the soul
Or how things may go
After you die,
Ask for the son of Pausanias,
Clan of Ptolemy.
You will find him
With the reverent people.

Ἢν δίζῃ Τίμαρχον ἐν Ἄϊδος, ὄφρα πύθηαι
ἤ τι περὶ ψυχῆς, ἢ πάλι πῶς ἔσεαι,
δίζεσθαι φυλῆς Πτολεμαΐδος, υἱέα πατρὸς
Παυσανίου· δήεις δ᾽αὐτὸν ἐν εὐσεβέων.

Callimachus

I was Demeter's priestess, then the Cabiris', then
Cybele's.
A crone now ash and dust, I say farewell.
Back then I oversaw the schooling of all the new
young girls.
I bore two sons. I closed my eyes in old age in
their arms.

Ἱερέη Δήμητρος ἐγώ ποτε, καὶ πάλιν Καβείρων,
ὦνερ, καὶ μετέπειτα Δινδυμήνης,
ἡ γρῆϋς γενόμην, ἡ νῦν κόνις, ἡνο...
πολλῶν προστασίη νέων γυναικῶν.
καί μοι τέκν᾽ ἐγένοντο δύ᾽ ἄρσενα, κἠπέμυσ᾽
ἐκείνων
εὐγήρως ἐνὶ χερσίν. ἕρπε χαίρων.

Callimachus

I wish fast ships had never been invented.
We wouldn't be standing here now
Mourning Sopolis, Diokleides' son.

His homeless corpse floats lost at sea
While we bow our heads in passing,
Not to him—to a name on an empty tomb.

Ὤφελε μηδ' ἐγένοντο θοαὶ νέες· οὐ γὰρ ἂν ἡμεῖς
    παῖδα Διοκλείδου Σώπολιν ἐστένομεν·
νῦν δ' ὁ μὲν εἰν ἁλί που φέρεται νέκυς· ἀντὶ δ'
        ἐκείνου
    οὔνομα καὶ κενεὸν σῆμα παρερχόμεθα.

Callimachus

Who *are* you, shipwrecked stranger?
Leontichus found you dead here on the beach
And heaped earth into a tomb this way
Shedding tears for his own short life,
Because he also never rests,
Ranging on the ocean like a seagull.

Τίς, ξένος ὦ ναυηγέ; Λεόντιχος ἐνθάδε νεκρὸν
εὗρέ σ' ἐπ' αἰγιαλοῦ, χῶσε δὲ τῷδε τάφῳ,
δακρύσας ἐπίκηρον ἑὸν βίον· οὐδὲ γὰρ αὐτὸς
ἥσυχος, αἰθυίῃ δ' ἶσα θαλασσοπορεῖ.

Callimachus

Someone mentioned your death today,
Heracleitus, and it brought me to tears,
Remembering how often we used to watch
The sun go down while we sat talking.
Now, old friend, you lie somewhere
Turned years ago to dust. Yet your verse
Lives on. And the god of death,
Who seizes everything, will never touch it!

Εἶπέ τίς, Ἡράκλειτε, τεὸν μόρον, ἐς δέ με δάκρυ
   ἤγαγεν, ἐμνήσθην δ᾽ ὁσσάκις ἀμφότεροι
ἥλιον ἐν λέσχῃ κατεδύσαμεν· ἀλλὰ σὺ μέν που,
   ξεῖν᾽ Ἁλικαρνησεῦ, τετράπαλαι σποδιή·
αἱ δὲ τεαὶ ζώουσιν ἀηδόνες, ᾗσιν ὁ πάντων
   ἁρπακτὴς Ἀΐδης οὐκ ἐπὶ χεῖρα βαλεῖ.

Anonymous Inscription
Third Century BCE

Stranger, should you reach Phthia one day
With its fine vineyards,
And come to old Thaumakia, my town,

Tell them there that climbing the desolate
Forests of Malea
You saw the grave of Derxias, Lampon's son,

Who, hurrying through here on his own,
Was tricked by thieves and jumped
From behind on his way to law-abiding Sparta.

Εἰπέ, ποτὶ Φθίαν εὐάμπελον ἤν ποθ' ἵκηαι
  καὶ πόλιν ἀρχαίαν, ὦ ξένε, Θαυμακίαν.
ὡς δρυμὸν Μαλεαῖον ἀναστείβων ποτ' ἔρημον
  εἶδες Λάμπωνος τόνδ' ἐπὶ παιδὶ τάφον
Δερξίᾳ, ὅν ποτε μοῦνον ἕλον δόλῳ, οὐδ' ἀναφανδόν,
  κλῶπες ἐπὶ Σπάρταν δῖαν ἐπειγόμενον.

Philetas of Samos

This stone weighed down with grief describes
How *Death has dragged off little Theodotia.*
One line below, the short-lived daughter speaks:
Father, don't weep. Humans are prone to misfortune.

Ἁ στάλα βαρύθουσα λέγει τάδε· "Τὰν μινύωρον,
τὰν μικκὰν Ἀΐδας ἅρπασε Θειοδόταν."
χἀ μικκὰ τάδε πατρὶ λέγει πάλιν· " Ἴσχεο λύπας,
Θειόδοτε· θνατοὶ πολλάκι δυστυχέες."

Damagetus

Phokaia, splendid city,
Here is the last thing Theano said
As she stepped back into the barren night:

"Darling Apellichus, I am so unhappy.
What sea are you crossing now in your swift
ship, Love?
Death stands by me.
I really should have died holding your hand."

Ὑστάτιον, Φώκαια, κλυτὴ πόλι, τοῦτο Θεανὼ
εἶπεν ἐς ἀτρύγετον νύκτα κατερχομένη·
"Οἴμοι ἐγὼ δύστηνος· Ἀπέλλιχε, ποῖον, ὅμευνε,
ποῖον ἐπ᾽ ὠκείῃ νηῒ περᾷς πέλαγος;
αὐτὰρ ἐμεῦ σχεδόθεν μόρος ἵσταται. ὡς ὄφελόν γε
χειρὶ φίλην τὴν σὴν χεῖρα λαβοῦσα θανεῖν."

Dioscorides

I, Thespis, gave tragic plays their shape,
Inventing a new diversion for my neighbors

Back in the days when, every third autumn
The god of wine led the chorus in

And the prize was a goat
And a basket of figs from Attica.

Now, young men reshape these things
And each new age will dream up more.

What's mine is mine.

Θέσπις ὅδε, τραγικὴν ὃς ἀνέπλασε πρῶτος ἀοιδὴν
  κωμήταις νεαρὰς καινοτομῶν χάριτας,
Βάκχος ὅτε τριετῆ κατάγοι χορόν, ᾧ τράγος ἄθλων
  χὠττικὸς ἦν σύκων ἄρριχος ἆθλον ἔτι.
οἱ δὲ μεταπλάσσουσι νέοι τάδε· μυρίος αἰὼν
  πολλὰ προσευρήσει χἄτερα· τἀμὰ δ' ἐμά.

Hegesippus

Some fishermen hauled up a half-eaten
Man, caught in a net full of flounder–
Wept-for remains of a lost voyage.

Rather than profit from ruin,
They buried the man and the fish in shallow
  sand.

Earth, here you have the whole shipwrecked man
Though, in place of the rest of his flesh,
You have those that ate it.

Ἐξ ἁλὸς ἡμίβρωτον ἀνηνέγκαντο σαγηνεῖς
  ἄνδρα, πολύκλαυτον ναυτιλίης σκύβαλον·
κέρδεα δ' οὐκ ἐδίωξαν ἃ μὴ θέμις· ἀλλὰ σὺν αὐτοῖς
  ἰχθύσι τῇδ' ὀλίγῃ θῆκαν ὑπὸ ψαμάθῳ.
ὦ χθών, τὸν ναυηγὸν ἔχεις ὅλον· ἀντὶ δὲ λοιπῆς
  σαρκὸς τοὺς σαρκῶν γευσαμένους ἐπέχεις.

Hegesippus

They say that Hermes
Leads good men
From the funeral pyre
To the underworld,
Past Rhadamanthys
Judge of the Dead,
Taking the path
On the right-hand side
By which Aristonous,
The son
Chaerestratus wept for,
Went down to
The house of Hades,
Commander of the dead.

Τὴν ἀπὸ πυρκαϊῆς ἐνδέξια φασὶ κέλευθον
  Ἑρμῆν τοὺς ἀγαθοὺς εἰς Ῥαδάμανθυν ἄγειν,
ᾗ καὶ Ἀριστόνοος, Χαιρεστράτου οὐκ ἀδάκρυτος
  παῖς, ἡγησίλεω δῶμ᾽ Ἀΐδος κατέβη.

Theaetetus

Flames (and no alarm) one winter night
Consumed the great house of Antagoras
While everyone inside lay drunk on wine.

Free men and servants, eighty souls in all
Died in the fire.
Their kinsmen couldn't tell the bones apart.

They had one urn, one funeral, one headstone.
Even so, the King of the Dead
Will pick out each of them among the ashes.

Χείματος οἰνωθέντα τὸν Ἀνταγόρεω μέγαν οἶκον
   ἐκ νυκτῶν ἔλαθεν πῦρ ὑπονειμάμενον·
ὀγδώκοντα δ' ἀριθμὸν ἐλεύθεροι ἄμμιγα δούλοις
   τῆς ἐχθρῆς ταύτης πυρκαϊῆς ἔτυχον.
οὐκ εἶχον διελεῖν προσκηδέες ὀστέα χωρίς·
   ξυνὴ δ' ἦν κάλπις, ξυνὰ δὲ τὰ κτέρεα·
εἷς καὶ τύμβος ἀνέστη· ἀτὰρ τὸν ἕκαστον ἐκείνων
   οἶδε καὶ ἐν τέφρῃ ῥηϊδίως Ἀΐδης.

Theaetetus

Sailors on the open sea,
Ariston of Cyrene asks
You, in the name of Zeus,
Guardian of strangers,
To tell my father Menon
That his son
Gave up the ghost
On the Aegean
And lies buried near the rocks
In Icaria.

Ναυτίλοι ὦ πλώοντες, ὁ Κυρηναῖος Ἀρίστων
πάντας ὑπὲρ Ξενίου λίσσεται ὔμμε Διός,
εἰπεῖν πατρὶ Μένωνι, παρ' Ἰκαρίαις ὅτι πέτραις
κεῖται, ἐν Αἰγαίῳ θυμὸν ἀφεὶς πελάγει.

Heracleitus

The earth is fresh. Wilting garlands
Flutter on the faces of these gravestones.
Decipher the letters, Traveler.
Let's see whose bones these were:

Stranger, I am Aretemias from Nidus,
Wife of Euphron.
I did not survive my labor.

Bearing twins, I left one son
To guide my husband through old age
And took one with me to remind me of him.

Ἀ κόνις ἀρτίσκαπτος, ἐπὶ στάλας δὲ μετώπων
  σείονται φύλλων ἡμιθαλεῖς στέφανοι·
γράμμα διακρίναντες, ὁδοιπόρε, πέτρον ἴδωμεν,
  λευρὰ περιστέλλειν ὀστέα φατὶ τίνος.—
"Ξεῖν', Ἀρετημιάς εἰμι· πάτρα Κνίδος· Εὔφρονος ἦλθον
  εἰς λέχος· ὠδίνων οὐκ ἄμορος γενόμαν·
δισσὰ δ' ὁμοῦ τίκτουσα, τὸ μὲν λίπον ἀνδρὶ ποδηγὸν
  γήρως· ὅν δ' ἀπάγω μναμόσυνον πόσιος."

Rhianus

Dust, send up a thorn tree to entwine me
Or raise a bramble's twisting arms,
So even springtime sparrows
Can't set their tiny feet on me.

Leave me in peace and quiet:
I, Timon, man with a bitter tongue,
Disliked by my neighbors, am cast out
Even here among the dead.

Τρηχεῖαν κατ' ἐμεῦ, ψαφαρὴ κόνι, ῥάμνον ἑλίσσοις
  πάντοθεν, ἢ σκολιῆς ἄγρια κῶλα βάτου,
ὡς ἐπ' ἐμοὶ μηδ' ὄρνις ἐν εἴαρι κοῦφον ἐρείδοι
  ἴχνος, ἐρημάζω δ' ἥσυχα κεκλιμένος.
ἦ γὰρ ὁ μισάνθρωπος, ὁ μηδ' ἀστοῖσι φιληθεὶς
  Τίμων οὐδ' Ἀΐδῃ γνήσιός εἰμι νέκυς.

Theodoridas:
A Marker on a Rocky Point

I am the grave of a shipwrecked man.
Stranger, sail away from me.
The day we died, the other boats
Stayed safely out to sea.

Ναυηγοῦ τάφος εἰμί· σὺ δὲ πλέε· καὶ γὰρ ὅθ' ἡμεῖς
ὠλλύμεθ', αἱ λοιπαὶ νῆες ἐποντοπόρουν.

Anonymous

Ariston eked out his living with a sling,
Stoning geese by stealing up
As they pecked his scattered seed
With sidelong glances.

Now he lies in the underworld.
Without a hand to whirl and make it sing,
The sling lies silent.
The geese fly south over his tomb.

Εἶχε κορωνοβόλον πενίης λιμηρὸν Ἀρίστων
 ὄργανον, ᾧ πτηνὰς ἠκροβόλιζε χένας,
ἧκα παραστείχων δολίην ὁδόν, οἷος ἐκείνας
ψεύσασθαι λοξοῖς ὄμμασι φερβομένας.
νῦν δ᾽ ὁ μὲν εἰν ἀΐδῃ· τὸ δέ οἱ βέλος ὀρφανὸν ἤχου
 καὶ χερός· ἡ δ᾽ ἄγρη τύμβον ὑπερπέταται.

Carphyllides

Stranger, don't mourn *me.* Pass by this tomb.
Even dead, I have nothing worth lamenting.
I enjoyed one woman, who grew old with me.
We had three children. They married. More
Young ones arrived as time went on. I rocked
them
To sleep on my lap, never losing one
To grief or illness. When my own end came,
The whole clan poured libations over me,
Sending me off on a painless journey. Now,
I sleep a sweet sleep in hallowed ground.

Μὴ μέμψῃ παριὼν τὰ μνήματά μου, παροδῖτα·
οὐδὲν ἔχω θρήνων ἄξιον οὐδὲ θανών.
τέκνων τέκνα λέλοιπα· μιῆς ἀπέλαυσα γυναικὸς
συγγήρου· τρισσοῖς παισὶν ἔδωκα γάμους,
ἐξ ὧν πολλάκι παῖδας ἐμοῖς ἐνεκοίμισα κόλποις,
οὐδενὸς οἰμώξας οὐ νόσον, οὐ θάνατον,
οἵ με κατασπείσαντες ἀπήμονα, τὸν γλυκὺν ὕπνον
κοιμᾶσθαι, χώρην πέμψαν ἐπ' εὐσεβέων.

Dionysius of Andros

Drenched with rain by Zeus
And soaked by Bacchus,
No wonder I took a spill and died.
It was two against one,
A man versus the gods.

Καὶ Διῒ καὶ Βρομίῳ με διάβροχον οὐ μέγ᾽ ὀλισθεῖν,
καὶ μόνον ἐκ δοιῶν, καὶ βροτὸν ἐκ μακάρων.

Chaeremon

Eubolus, Athanagoras's son:
Least fortunate of men,
Most widely praised.

Εὔβουλον τέκνωσεν Ἀθηναγόρης περὶ πάντων
ἥσσονα μὲν μοίρᾳ, κρέσσονα δ' εὐλογίᾳ.

Chaeremon

We Spartans fought the Argives here, matching them man
For man and spear to spear for the prize of Thyreae.
Since both sides freely gave up all hope of going home,
We leave the job of reporting our death to the crows.

Τοῖς Ἄργει Σπάρτηθεν ἴσαι χέρες, ἶσα δὲ τεύχη
συμβάλομεν· Θυρέαι δ᾽ ἦσαν ἄεθλα δορός.
ἄμφω δ᾽ ἀπροφάσιστα τὸν οἴκαδε νόστον ἀφέντες
οἰωνοῖς θανάτου λείπομεν ἀγγελίαν.

Antipater of Sidon

This patch of ground in Asia holds Phillip's son,
  Amyntor,
A soldier made tough by iron war.
No painful sickness dragged him down to the
  house of darkness.
He died holding his shield over a friend.

Λύδιον οὖδας ἔχει τόδ' Ἀμύντορα, παῖδα Φιλίππου,
  πολλὰ σιδηρείης χερσὶ θιγόντα μάχης·
οὐδέ μιν ἀλγινόεσσα νόσος δόμον ἄγαγε Νυκτός,
  ἀλλ' ὄλετ' ἀμφ' ἑτάρῳ σχὼν κυκλόεσσαν ἴτυν.

Antipater of Sidon

Orpheus, you will never guide
The spellbound oaks and rocks again,
Or herd wild beasts foraging on their own.

Nor will you still another wind
Howling with hail and slantwise snow,
Or calm another roaring sea.

You are dead and gone
And the Muses mourn you,
Led by great Calliope, your mother.

Why do we cry for our lost sons,
When even the gods can't
Save their own from dying?

Οὐκέτι θελγομένας, Ὀρφεῦ, δρύας, οὐκέτι πέτρας
ἄξεις, οὐ θηρῶν αὐτονόμους ἀγέλας·
οὐκέτι κοιμάσεις ἀνέμων βρόμον, οὐχὶ χάλαζαν,
οὐ νιφετῶν συρμούς, οὐ παταγεῦσαν ἅλα.
ὤλεο γάρ· σὲ δὲ πολλὰ κατωδύραντο θύγατρες
Μναμοσύνας, μάτηρ δ' ἔξοχα Καλλιόπα.
τί φθιμένοις στοναχεῦμεν ἐφ' υἱάσιν, ἁνίκ' ἀλαλκεῖν
τῶν παίδων Ἀΐδην οὐδὲ θεοῖς δύναμις;

Antipater of Sidon

Hipparchia chose the hard life of the Cynics
Over a woman's work in flowing robes.

No tunics pinned with brooches, no soft
  slippers,
No hair net with slick pomade for me.

I'll take a sack and a walking stick,
A thick cloak, a bedroll on the ground.

My legacy will outstrip swift Atalanta,
As wisdom beats racing through the hills.

Οὐχὶ βαθυστόλμων Ἱππαρχία ἔργα γυναικῶν,
  τῶν δὲ Κυνῶν ἑλόμαν ῥωμαλέον βίοτον·
οὐδέ μοι ἀμπεχόναι περονήτιδες, οὐ βαθύπελμος
  εὐμαρίς, οὐ λιπόων εὔαδε κεκρύφαλος·
οὐλὰς δὲ σκίπωνι συνέμπορος, ἅ τε συνῳδὸς
  δίπλαξ, καὶ κοίτας βλῆμα χαμαιλεχέος.
ἄμμι δὲ Μαιναλίας κάρρων †ἄμιν Ἀταλάντας
  τόσσον, ὅσον σοφία κρέσσον ὀριδρομίας.

Diotimos

The cows came down on their own tonight,
Trudging along through heavy snow,
While up on the summit, Therimachus
Lies stretched under the oaks,
Laid out by a lightning bolt from heaven.

Αὐτόμαται δείλῃ ποτὶ ταὔλιον αἱ βόες ἦλθον
ἐξ ὄρεος, πολλῇ νιφόμεναι χίονι·
αἰαῖ, Θηρίμαχος δὲ παρὰ δρυῒ τὸν μακρὸν εὕδει
ὕπνον· ἐκοιμήθη δ' ἐκ πυρὸς οὐρανίου.

IV

The Millennium

Pagan Roman Empire, 100 BCE–99 CE

In the centuries flanking the millennium, writing Greek epigrams became a well-established profession. The form served widespread public needs and in some cases even supported its practitioners. A prolific epigrammatist might earn a living composing dedications for fountains, stairs, walls, temples and public buildings, and by supplying epitaphs to families of deceased Greeks. Some of these poets gained positions at court or were appointed as salaried scholars or librarians. Already in the third century BCE, Posidippus could write that his calling produced the wherewithal to leave "both home and wealth" to his descendants.

Anthologists flourished too, gathering selected verses from the ephemeral collections of poetry past and present. Epigrams of all sorts were popular, and selections on scrolls for the personal library were a natural development. Among these early anthologies, the most influential by far was Meleager's *Garland*. Over the next thousand years, subsequent editors drew on this work above all others to develop the Greek Anthology we read today.

Born in Gadara in Palestine, raised in Syrian Tyre, later a citizen of the Phoenician community on Kos, Meleager was both an inspired poet and a first-rate editor. His 134 extant epigrams display a comprehensive knowledge of the tradition his anthology preserved. Arranging earlier poets' works by theme and subtheme, he often rounded off a selection with epigrams of his own that occasionally outshone his predecessors'. Meleager's best epigrams strike a personal, confiding tone that communicates easily to modern readers. The direction he took defined the form's course for centuries.

The Roman Empire's rapid expansion in this period subsumed and refigured the spirit of ancient Greece. The reading of Greek remained a hallmark of cultured Romans, and good Greek literature continued to be made. The epigram was advanced in fresh, new ways. Lucilius, for example, introduced the use of hyperbolic humor, employing exaggeration to sharpen the form's satiric edge. Nicarchus, a contemporary, followed suit. The incompetent physician on page 140, whose examination precipitates the death of a statue, is typical. This accent on acerbic wit opened new terrain for the epigram and influenced the Latin satirist Martial.

Anonymous

After what happened to you, Theogenes,
Men should swear off seafaring forever.

The Libyan deep became your grave
When a thousand cranes, searching for land,

Found your loaded ship instead
And, settling in the rigging wing to wing,

Sent it to the bottom of the ocean.

Πάντα τις ἀρήσαιτο φυγεῖν πλόον, ὁππότε καὶ σύ,
  Θεῦγενες, ἐν Λιβυκῷ τύμβον ἔθευ πελάγει,
ἡνίκα σοι κεκμηὸς ἐπέπτατο φορτίδι νηῒ
  οὖλον ἀνηρίθμων κεῖνο νέφος γεράνων.

Meleager

My father was Eucrates.
Meleager is my name.
Born in Gadara, Palestine
I came of age in Tyre.

A Syrian?
Don't be surprised.
All men share one homeland
Called the World.

If you're Syrian, *Salam!*
If Phoenician, *Haudoni!*
If Greek, then *Chaîre!*
Hail! And wish

The ancient babbler well.
May you
When you grow old
Be this loquacious!

(I wrote these lines in my notebook
Before they buried me.
Old age and death
Are next-door neighbors.)

Νᾶσος ἐμὰ θρέπτειρα Τύρος· πάτρα δέ με τεκνοῖ
  Ἀτθὶς ἐν Ἀσσυρίοις ναιομένα, Γάδαρα·
Εὐκράτεω δ' ἔβλαστον ὁ σὺν Μούσαις Μελέαγρος
  πρῶτα Μενιππείοις συντροχάσας Χάρισιν.
εἰ δὲ Σύρος, τί τὸ θαῦμα; μίαν, ξένε, πατρίδα κόσμον
  ναίομεν· ἓν θνατοὺς πάντας ἔτικτε Χάος.
πουλυετὴς δ' ἐχάραξα τάδ' ἐν δέλτοισι πρὸ τύμβου·
  γήρως γὰρ γείτων ἐγγύθεν Ἀΐδεω.
ἀλλά με τὸν λαλιὸν καὶ πρεσβύτην προτιειπὼν
  χαίρειν, εἰς γῆρας καὐτὸς ἵκοιο λάλον.

Meleager

In place of a husband Clearista met
The god of death on her wedding night
Just as she was loosening her clothes.

The chamber doors had just banged shut.
The bedtime flutes rang through the house.
The same flutes raised a wail at sunrise.

The dampened wedding song turned to a groan.
Then torches that had flared around the
  bedroom
Lit her way on the downward-running road.

Οὐ γάμον, ἀλλ' Ἀΐδαν ἐπινυμφίδιον Κλεαρίστα
  δέξατο, παρθενίας ἅμματα λυομένα.
ἄρτι γὰρ ἑσπέριοι νύμφας ἐπὶ δικλίσιν ἄχευν
  λωτοί, καὶ θαλάμων ἐπλαταγεῦντο θύραι·
ἠῷοι δ' ὀλολυγμὸν ἀνέκραγον, ἐκ δ' Ὑμέναιος
  σιγαθεὶς γοερὸν φθέγμα μεθαρμόσατο·
αἱ δ' αὐταὶ καὶ φέγγος ἐδᾳδούχουν παρὰ παστῷ
  πεῦκαι, καὶ φθιμένᾳ νέρθεν ἔφαινον ὁδόν.

Anonymous

Cleo, your hair was never cut
Nor had the moon run down
The sky three dozen times,
When your mother and father
Leaned above you,
Howling over your coffin.
You will reach your prime in unknown Acheron.
You will never come back here.

Οὔπω τοι πλόκαμοι τετμημένοι, οὐδὲ σελάνας
  τοὶ τριετεῖς μηνῶν ἀνιοχεῦντο δρόμοι,
Κλεύδικε, Νικασὶς ὅτε σὰν περὶ λάρνακα μάτηρ,
  τλῆμον, ἐπ' αἰακτᾷ πόλλ' ἐβόα στεφάνᾳ,
καὶ γενέτας Περίκλειτος· ἐπ' ἀγνώτῳ δ' Ἀχέροντι
  ἡβάσεις ἥβαν, Κλεύδικ', ἀνοστοτάταν.

Zonas of Sardis

Charon, cloaked in darkness,
Before you row death's ship
Through the reeds to Hades,
Steady the ladder.

Reach out a hand for the son of Cinyras.
Help him aboard.
He is too young to walk well in sandals
And frightened to touch the sand with his
bare feet.

Ἀΐδη ὅς ταύτης καλαμώδεος ὕδατι λίμνης
κωπεύεις νεκύων βᾶριν, †ἐλῶν ὀδύνην,
τῷ Κινύρου τὴν χεῖρα βατηρίδος ἐμβαίνοντι
κλίμακος ἐκτείνας, δέξο, κελαινὲ Χάρον·
πλάζει γὰρ τὸν παῖδα τὰ σάνδαλα· γυμνὰ δὲ θεῖναι
ἴχνια δειμαίνει ψάμμον ἔπ' ᾐονίην.

Nicomachus

This (why bother to call it 'this')
Was once the town of Plataea,
Before a sudden quake
Knocked it all down.

Scarcely anyone was left:
Only a little rise, and we, the dead,
With the place we loved
Laid on top of us.

Ἁδ' ἔσθ'– ἅδε Πλάταια τί τοι λέγω;– ἅν ποτε σεισμὸς
ἐλθὼν ἐξαπίνας κάββαλε πανσυδίῃ·
λείφθη δ' αὖ μοῦνον τυτθὸν γένος· οἱ δὲ θανόντες
σᾶμ' ἐρατὰν πάτραν κείμεθ' ἐφεσσάμενοι.

Tymnes

This headstone marks a white Maltese.
All his life they called him Bull.
He guarded Eumelus faithfully.
Now, night's silent roads
Have swallowed up his barking.

Τῇδε τὸν ἐκ Μελίτης ἀργὸν κύνα φησὶν ὁ πέτρος
ἴσχειν, Εὐμήλου πιστότατον φύλακα.
Ταῦρόν μιν καλέεσκον, ὅτ᾽ ἦν ἔτι· νῦν δὲ τὸ κείνου
φθέγμα σιωπηραὶ νυκτὸς ἔχουσιν ὁδοί.

Serapion of Alexandria

This bone was part of a working man:
You either sold goods in the market
Or fished on dark, uncertain seas.

Tell those to come
How, chasing other prospects,
Everyone will be reduced to this.

Τοῦτ’ ὀστεῦν φωτὸς πολυεργέος. ἦ ῥά τις ἦσθα
 ἔμπορος, ἢ τυφλοῦ κύματος ἰχθυβόλος.
ἄγγειλον θνητοῖσιν ὅτι σπεύδοντες ἐς ἄλλας
 ἐλπίδας εἰς τοίην ἐλπίδα λυόμεθα.

Antiphilus of Byzantium

Old Philo bent to lift a corpse
(He earned his living doing this)
And missed a step and fell and died.
Well, he was ready. Old age
And death lay in wait for him.
The same pallet that bore so many others
He shouldered without knowing for himself.

Νεκροδόκον κλιντῆρα Φίλων ὁ πρέσβυς ἀείρων
ἐγκλιδόν, ὄφρα λάβοι μισθὸν ἐφημέριον,
σφάλματος ἐξ ὀλίγοιο πεσὼν θάνεν· ἦν γὰρ ἕτοιμος
εἰς ἀΐδην, ἐκάλει δ’ ἡ πολιὴ πρόφασιν·
ὃν δ’ἄλλοις ἐφόρει νεκυοστόλον, αὐτὸς ἐφ’ αὑτῷ
ἀσκάντην ὁ γέρων ἀχθοφορῶν ἔλαθεν.

Antiphilus of Byzantium

These two sons of Oedipus–
Heap their tombs up far apart.

Even death can't end their disagreements.
They refused to share a boat to Acheron.

Though they are dead
The god of war burns bright in them.

See how even the flame of their pyre
Breaks into a pair of bickering tongues!

Τηλοτάτω χεύασθαι ἔδει τάφον Οἰδιπόδαο
  παισὶν ἀπ᾽ ἀλλήλων, οἷς πέρας οὐ δ᾽ Ἀΐδας·
ἀλλὰ καὶ εἰς Ἀχέροντος ἕνα πλόον ἠρνήσαντο,
  χὠ στυγερὸς ζώει κἠν φθιμένοισιν Ἄρης.
ἠνίδε πυρκαϊῆς ἄνισον φλόγα· δαιομένα γὰρ
  ἐξ ἑνὸς εἰς δισσὰν δῆριν ἀποστρέφεται.

Ariston

Old Ampelis, who loved her wine
Came leaning on a wooden cane

To sneak a drink from this year's vat.
She filled a cup fit for a Cyclops,

But before she could raise it
She lost her grip. Then like a ship

Swallowed by waves, she dropped
Into the wine-dark sea and vanished.

Euterpe set this stone up on her grave,
Near where the grape mash lies drying in the
sun.

Ἀμπελὶς ἡ φιλάκρητος ἐπὶ σκήπωνος ὁδηγοῦ
ἤδη τὸ σφαλερὸν γῆρας ἐρειδομένη,
λαθριδίη Βάκχοιο νεοθλιβὲς ἦρ’ ἀπὸ ληνοῦ
πῶμα Κυκλωπείην πλησομένη κύλικα·
πρὶν δ’ ἀρύσαι μογερὰν ἔκαμεν χέρα· γραῦς δὲ
παλαιή,
ναῦς ἅθ’ ὑποβρύχιος ζωρὸν ἔδυ πέλαγος.
Εὐτέρπη δ’ ἐπὶ τύμβῳ ἀποφθιμένης θέτο σῆμα
λάϊνον, οἰνηρῶν γείτονα θειλοπέδων.

Erinagoras

Wretched to be snared this way,
Reckless, self-certain,
Ignoring the trickster Death:

Take Seleucus, perfect in word and deed,
Who after a short-lived burst of youth
Lies estranged at the world's edge,

Here on the unmapped Spanish coast
Far from his native Lesbos.

Δείλαιοι, τί κεναῖσιν ἀλώμεθα θαρσήσαντες
  ἐλπίσιν, ἀτηροῦ ληθόμενοι θανάτου;
ἦν ὅδε καὶ μύθοισι καὶ ἤθεσι πάντα Σέλευκος
  ἄρτιος, ἀλλ' ἥβης βαιὸν ἐπαυρόμενος,
ὑστατίοις ἐν Ἴβηρσι, τόσον δίχα τηλόθι Λέσβου,
  κεῖται ἀμετρήτων ξεῖνος ἐπ' αἰγιαλῶν.

Anonymous:
A Field

Once I was the field of Achaemenides.
Now I belong to Menippus.
I will keep moving forever
From one man's hand to the next.
Achaemenides thought he owned me.
Now Menippus thinks the same.
I don't belong to anyone but Fortune.

Ἀγρὸς Ἀχαιμενίδου γενόμην ποτέ, νῦν δὲ Μενίππου·
καὶ πάλιν ἐξ ἑτέρου βήσομαι εἰς ἕτερον.
καὶ γὰρ ἐκεῖνος ἔχειν μέ ποτ' ᾤετο, καὶ πάλιν οὗτος
οἴεται· εἰμὶ δ' ὅλως οὐδενός, ἀλλὰ Τύχης.

Antipater of Thessalonica

Don't judge a man by his headstone.
This one may not look like much,
But it marks a great man's bones.

Remember Alcman, master lyrist,
Ranked first by all nine Muses?
Here he lies,

A point of contention between two continents–
Claimed by Greece as Spartan, by Asia as Lydian.
Lyric poets may have many mothers.

Ἀνέρα μὴ πέτρῃ τεκμαίρεο. λιτὸς ὁ τύμβος
  ὀφθῆναι, μεγάλου δ' ὀστέα φωτὸς ἔχει.
εἰδήσεις Ἀλκμᾶνα, λύρης ἐλατῆρα Λακαίνης
  ἔξοχον, ὃν Μουσέων ἐννέ' ἀριθμὸς ἔχει·
κεῖται δ' ἠπείροις διδύμοις ἔρις, εἴθ' ὅγε Λυδός,
  εἴτε Λάκων· πολλαὶ μητέρες ὑμνοπόλων.

Antipater of Thessalonica

I'm not sure which to blame,
The god of wine or god of rain.
Either one may trip you up.

This tomb holds Polyxenus.
Returning from a banquet in the country,
He tumbled to his death down a slick hill.

He lies a long way from Smyrna now.
Let every drunk on the road after dark
Avoid the rain-soaked trail.

Οὐκ οἶδ' εἰ Διόνυσον ὀνόσσομαι, ἢ Διὸς ὄμβρον
μέμψομ'· ὀλίσθηροὶ δ' εἰς πόδας ἀμφότεροι.
ἀγρόθε γὰρ κατιόντα Πολύξενον ἔκ ποτε δαιτὸς
τύμβος ἔχει γλίσχρων ἐξεριπόντα λόφων·
κεῖται δ' Αἰολίδος Σμύρνης ἑκάς. ἀλλά τις ὄρφνης
δειμαίνοι μεθύων ἀτραπὸν ὑετίην.

Antipater of Thessalonica

All seas are the same. We're fools
To blame the Cyclades,
The Hellespont or Bay of Locri.
They don't deserve it.
How else could I escape them all
Before Scarfea Harbor's water
Closed over my head?
Pray for fair weather if you want.
The sea will be the sea.
Aristagoras, buried here, knows that.

Πᾶσα θάλασσα θάλασσα· τί Κυκλάδας ἢ στενὸν
    Ἕλλης
  κῦμα καὶ Ὀξείας ἠλεὰ μεμφόμεθα;
ἄλλως τοὔνομ' ἔχουσιν· ἐπεὶ τί με, τὸν προφυγόντα
  κεῖνα, Σκαρφαιεὺς ἀμφεκάλυψε λιμήν;
νόστιμον εὐπλοΐην ἀρῴτό τις· ὡς τά γε πόντου
  πόντος, ὁ τυμβευθεὶς οἶδεν Ἀρισταγόρης.

Antipater of Thessalonica

Melting snow up on the roof
Caved it in and killed old Lysidice.
Her neighbors didn't dig a grave. Instead,
They made the house her mausoleum.

Χειμερίου νιφετοῖο περὶ θριγκοῖσι τακέντος
  δῶμα πεσὸν τὴν γραῦν ἔκτανε Λυσιδίκην·
σῆμα δέ οἱ κωμῆται ὁμώλακες οὐκ ἀπ' ὀρυκτῆς
  γαίης, ἀλλ' αὐτὸν πύργον ἔθεντο τάφον.

Apollonides

I am a pile of pebbles on the shore,
Covering the skeleton of Glenis.
He stood fishing from an outcrop
When a rogue wave swept him off.
Those he worked with placed me here.
Protect them, Poseidon.
Give all who cast their lines a quiet shore.

Γλῆνιν παρῃονῖτις ἀμφέχω χερμάς,
πικρῇ κατασπασθέντα κύματος δίνῃ,
ὅτ' ἰχθυάζετ' ἐξ ἄκρης ἀπορρῶγος·
χῶσαν δέ μ' ὅσσος λαὸς ἦν συνεργήτης,
Πόσειδον, οὓς σὺ σῶζε, καὶ γαληναίην
αἰὲν διδοίης ὁρμιηβόλοις θῖνα.

Apollonides

Heliodorus went first. An hour later
His wife Diogenia followed.
They lived together.
Now they lie beneath one stone.
Once they gladly shared a bed.
Now they share this tomb.

Ἔφθανεν Ἡλιόδωρος, ἐφέσπετο δ', οὐδ' ὅσον ὥρῃ
ὕστερον, ἀνδρὶ φίλῳ Διογένεια δάμαρ.
ἄμφω δ', ὡς ἅμ' ἔναιον, ὑπὸ πλακὶ τυμβεύονται,
ξυνὸν ἀγαλλόμενοι καὶ τάφον ὡς θάλαμον.

Anonymous

I, Callicrateia, bore twenty-nine children.
Not one son or daughter died before me.
I lived to be a hundred and five and
Never set a shaking hand upon a cane.

Εἴκοσι Καλλικράτεια καὶ ἐννέα τέκνα τεκοῦσα,
οὐδ' ἑνὸς οὐδὲ μιῆς ἐδρακόμην θάνατον·
ἀλλ' ἑκατὸν καὶ πέντε διηνυσάμην ἐνιαυτούς,
σκίπωνι τρομερὰν οὐκ ἐπιθεῖσα χέρα.

Etruscus of Messene

The same boat, doing double duty,
Ferried Hieroclides to work

And down to Hades. It brought him fish
And served him as a pyre.

It sailed with him on the chase
And accompanied him to Hades.

Fortunate angler,
He cruised the sea in his own vessel

And then raced off
To the underworld in it.

Ἡ μία καὶ βιότοιο καὶ Ἄϊδος ἤγαγεν εἴσω
   ναῦς Ἱεροκλείδην, κοινὰ λαχοῦσα τέλη.
ἔτρεφεν ἰχθυβολεῦντα, κατέφλεγε τεθνειῶτα,
   σύμπλοος εἰς ἄγρην, σύμπλοος εἰς Ἀΐδην.
ὄλβιος ὁ γριπεὺς ἰδίῃ καὶ πόντον ἐπέπλει
   νηΐ, καὶ ἐξ ἰδίης ἔδραμεν εἰς Ἀΐδην.

Leonidas of Alexandria

"Who is the Argive spirit in this tomb?
Is he a brother of Dikaeoteles?"
  –*A brother of Dikaeoteles.*
"Was that an echo, or the real voice of the man?"
  –*The real voice of the man.*

α. Τίς Δαίμων Ἀργεῖος ἐπ' ἠρίῳ; ἆρα σύναιμος
  ἐστὶ Δικαιοτέλους; β. Ἐστὶ Δικαιοτέλους.
α. Ἠχὼ τοῦτ' ἐλάλησε πανύστατον, ἢ τόδ' ἀληθές,
  κεῖνος ὅδ' ἐστὶν ἀνήρ; β. Κεῖνος ὅδ' ἐστὶν ἀνήρ.

Lucilius

A chorus of astrologers confirmed it:
My uncle would live to old age.

Only Hermoclides foresaw an early death,

But by then the corpse was laid out
And the family in mourning.

Τῷ πατρί μου τὸν ἀδελφὸν οἱ ἀστρολόγοι
μακρόγη ρων
πάντες ἐμαντεύσανθ' ὡς ἀφ' ἑνὸς στόματος·
ἀλλ' Ἑρμοκλείδης αὐτὸν μόνος εἶπε πρόμοιρον·
εἶπε δ', ὅτ' αὐτὸν ἔσω νεκρὸν ἐκοπτόμεθα.

Lucilius

Seeing beside him
A man hung on a higher cross than he,
Diophon the envious
Began to pine.

Μακροτέρῳ σταυρῷ σταυρούμενον ἄλλον ἑαυτοῦ
ὁ φθονερὸς Διοφῶν ἐγγὺς ἰδὼν ἐτάκη.

Lucilius

Hermon the miser hanged himself,
Wracked with grief that in his sleep
He dreamed he had spent some money.

Ποιήσας δαπάνην ἐν ὕπνοις ὁ φιλάργυρος Ἕρμων
ἐκ περιωδυνίας αὑτὸν ἀπηγχόνισεν.

Nicarchus

Yesterday, Dr. Markos checked the pulse of Zeus.
Today, though made of marble and king of the
  gods,
Zeus is being carted to the graveyard.

Τοῦ λιθίνου Διὸς ἐχθὲς ὁ κλινικὸς ἥψατο Μάρκος·
  καὶ λίθος ὢν καὶ Ζεύς, σήμερον ἐκφέρεται.

Philip of Thessalonica:
A Millstone

This miller owned me while he lived.
All through life I ground his wheat–
Demeter's servant, groaning as I turned.

When he died they set me on his tomb,
A sign of his guild and a weight to feel forever–
At work while he lived, and on his bones in
death.

Πυρηφάτον Δάματρος εὐκάρπου λάτριν,
καὶ κατθανὼν στάλωσε τῷδ' ἐπ' ἠρίῳ,
σύνθημα τέχνας· ὣς ἔχει μ' ἀεὶ βαρύν,
καὶ ζῶν ἐν ἔργοις, καὶ θανὼν ἐπ' ὀστέοις.

Anonymous Inscription

Here lies a woman famed throughout the land:
I only took my clothes off for one man.

Ἁ δ' ἐγὼ ἁ περίβωτος ὑπὸ πλακὶ τῇδε τέθαμμαι,
μούνῳ ἐνὶ ζώναν ἀνέρι λυσαμένα.

V

Late Antiquity

Christian Roman Empire, 200–599 CE

The Roman Emperor Constantine yoked the Classical world to Christianity early in the fourth century. In time, the imperial educational curriculum passed into theologians' hands. Under the double weight of religion and empire, the delicate epigram began to buckle. Its defining characteristics—independent vision and a passionate frankness concerning life's joys and sorrows—gave way to the churchly emphasis on renunciation and salvation. The effect, especially on the epitaph, proved fatal.

Everything did not collapse at once. Originality remained possible. Good epitaphs continued to be written for several more centuries, at times with flair, as this final section shows. Even late in the sixth century, a poem by Agathias (page 156), could successfully adopt the voice of a great house mourning its builder's death. Around the same time, Damaskios managed a convincing, two-line meditation on the death of a slave (page 160), but instances like these were growing rare.

Among resolutely pagan poets, effete refinement begins to replace compression. Among new Christians, heavy-handed moralizing more often stands in for real emotion, and conventional tropes supplant fresh similes. Palladas the Alexandrian, author of more than 150 epigrams, raises one of the last clear voices in Classicism's struggle with the Church. His art when compared to Callimachus's may seem crude, but his melancholy candor is impressive. Palladas earned his living as a professional teacher of Greek and Latin literature. In old age, he lost his livelihood to a series of Christian reforms and anti-pagan laws. Though he never embraced Christianity, he considered opposition to it futile. A truth-telling poet, he predicts the demise of the classical world, even penning its epitaph:

Latter-day Greeks, are we not dead
And only seem to be alive . . . ?

The closing of Plato's Academy in Athens in 529 marks the official end of Greek pedagogy. A center of learning for a thousand years, the Academy stood for a method of uncovering truth through logical disputation that the new theology rejected. Fittingly, the Academy's last director was the epigrammatist Damaskios. He fled to Persia after Emperor Justinian closed the school.

The work of the scholar Agathias (536–582) marks a dividing line in quality and subject matter. With few exceptions, the writing of first-rate elegiac epigrams ends with him in the late sixth century. After Agathias, most surviving examples are exercises in rhetoric or predictable formulations on conventional Christian themes.

Anonymous

If you notice this tomb at all as you pass,
Don't smirk because it only holds a dog.
I was wept for.
My master's hands heaped up this dirt,
Then cut these words into my stone.

Τὴν τρίβον ὃς παράγεις, ἄν πως τόδε σῆμα νοήσῃς
  μή, δέομαι, γελάσῃς εἰ κυνός ἐστι τάφος·
Ἐκλαύσθην· χεῖρες δὲ κόνιν συνέθηκαν ἄνακτος
  ὅς μου καὶ στήλῃ τὸνδ' ἐχάραξε λόγον.

Diogenes Laertius

Socrates, now you may drink in Zeus's house.
The oracle was right to call you wise.
Wisdom itself is a goddess.
All you got from the people of Athens was
  hemlock.
They swallowed it themselves when it touched
  your lips.

Πῖνέ νυν ἐν Διὸς ὤν, ὦ Σώκρατες· ἦ σε γὰρ ὄντως
  καὶ σοφὸν εἶπε θεός, καὶ θεὸς ἡ σοφία.
πρὸς γὰρ Ἀθηναίων κώνειον ἁπλῶς σὺ ἐδέξω,
  αὐτοὶ δ' ἐξέπιον τοῦτο τεῷ στόματι.

Diogenes Laertius

Eudoxus discovered his fate in Memphis.
A bull with pretty horns informed him.
It didn't speak—
How could it?
Cattle don't talk with their tongues.
It licked his robe instead, as if to say,
Your life is about to be stripped away.
He died soon after—fifty-three years old.

Ἐν Μέμφει λόγος ἐστὶ μαθεῖν ἰδίην ποτὲ μοίρην
Εὔδοξον παρὰ τοῦ καλλίκερω ταύρου·
κοὐδὲν ἔλεξε· πόθεν; βοῒ γὰρ λόγον οὐ πόρε φύτλη,
οὐδὲ λάλον μόσχῳ Ἄπιδι στόμα·
ἀλλὰ παρ' αὐτὸν λέχριος στὰς ἐλιχμήσατο στόλον,
προφανῶς τοῦτο διδάσκων· "Ἀποδύσῃ βιοτὴν
ὅσσον οὔπω." διὸ καί οἱ ταχέως ἦλθε μόρος, δεκάκις
πέντε καὶ τρεῖς εἰσιδόντα ποίας.

Palladas

Psullo, getting old, begrudged her heirs
And made herself sole beneficiary.
She stepped off to Hades in one quick leap,
Expending life and wealth at once.
She sank the estate and went down with it.
She jumped to her death
After spending the last penny.

Ψυλλὼ πρεσβυγενὴς τοῖς κληρονόμοις φθονέσασα,
  αὐτὴ κληρονόμος τῶν ἰδίων γέγονεν·
ἀλλομένη δὲ τάχος κατέβη δόμον εἰς Ἀΐδαο,
  ταῖς δαπάναις τὸ ζῆν σύμμετρον εὑρομένη.
πάντα φαγοῦσα βίον συναπώλετο ταῖς δαπάναισιν·
  ἥλατο δ' εἰς ἀΐδην, ὡς ἀπεκερμάτισεν.

Palladas

Latter-day Greeks, are we not dead
And only seem to be alive,
Having fallen on hard times,
Mistaking a dream for existence?
Or are we alive,
While our way of life has perished?

Ἆρα μὴ θανόντες τῷ δοκεῖν ζῶμεν μόνον,
Ἕλληνες ἄνδρες, συμφορᾷ πεπτωκότες
ὄνειρον εἰκάζοντες εἶναι τὸν βίον;
ἢ ζῶμεν ἡμεῖς, τοῦ βίου τεθνηκότος;

Julianos, Prefect of Egypt

Greetings, shipwrecked sailor: When you arrive
in Hades
Don't blame ocean waves for what the wind did.
Wind
Overwhelmed you. The gentle waters washed
you back
On shore, where your father and your
grandfathers lie buried.

Χαῖρέ μοι, ὦ ναυηγέ, καὶ εἰς Ἀΐδαο περήσας
μέμφεο μὴ πόντου κύμασιν, ἀλλ' ἀνέμοις.
κεῖνοι μέν σ' ἐδάμασσαν· ἁλὸς δέ σε μείλιχον ὕδωρ
ἐς χθόνα καὶ πατέρων ἐξεκύλισε τάφους.

Julianos, Prefect of Egypt

Neither the sea nor wild winds destroyed you.
It was your insatiable need to race around on
business.
Give me a modest living on dry land.
Let others wring big profits from the sea, battling
whirlwinds.

Οὔτι σε πόντος ὄλεσσε καὶ οὐ πνείοντες ἀῆται,
ἀλλ' ἀκόρητος ἔρως φοιτάδος ἐμπορίης.
εἴη μοι γαίης ὀλίγος βίος· ἐκ δὲ θαλάσσης
ἄλλοισιν μελέτω κέρδος ἀελλομάχον.

Julianos, Prefect of Egypt

Pyrro the skeptic, are you really dead?
  I doubt it.
After facing your fate, you still say this?
  I doubt it.
Well, your tomb has laid to rest your doubts.

α. Κάτθανες, ὦ Πύρρων; β. Ἐπέχω. α. Πυμάτην μετὰ μοῖραν
  φῂς ἐπέχειν; β. Ἐπέχω. α. Σκέψιν ἔπαυσε τάφος.

Julianos, Prefect of Egypt

Though the painter caught her looks perfectly,
It would be better if his skill had failed,
Letting us forget her face
Who still mourn Theodosia.

Αὐτὴν Θειοδότην ὁ ζωγράφος. αἴθε δὲ τέχνης
ἤμβροτε, καὶ λήθην δῶκεν ὀδυρομένοις.

Agathias Scholasticus: On a House in Byzantium

Musonius worked hard to put me up –
A big house and impressive too,

Built in the teeth of a harsh north wind. Still,
He could not escape fate's lightless room.

Abandoning me, he rests underground
Reclining on a narrow strip of earth,

While I, where he found joy,
Am home to strangers.

Τεῦξέ με πολλὰ καμὼν Μουσώνιος οἶκον ἀγητὸν
 τηλίκον, ἀρκτῴοις ἄσθμασι βαλλόμενον.
ἔμπης οὐκ ἀπέειπεν ἀφεγγέα δώματα Μοίρης,
 ἀλλά με καλλείψας ἐν χθονὶ ναιετάει.
καί ῥ' ὁ μὲν εἰς ὀλίγην κεῖται κόνιν· ἡ δὲ περισσὴ
 τέρψις ἐπὶ ξείνοις ἀνδράσιν ἐκκέχυμαι.

Agathias Scholasticus: A Riddle

This tomb holds no body.
This corpse has no grave.
It is its own corpse.
It is its own gravestone.

Ὁ τύμβος οὗτος ἔνδον οὐκ ἔχει νεκρόν·
ὁ νεκρὸς οὗτος ἐκτὸς οὐκ ἔχει τάφον,
ἀλλ᾽αὐτὸς αὑτοῦ νεκρός ἐστι καὶ τάφος.

Agathias Scholasticus

All night I weep alone in bed.
As I fall asleep at dawn,
The swallows stir. They wake me,
And I start to cry again.

I shut my eyes,
But Rhoda's features haunt me.
Birds, be quiet. I didn't stop
A dead young woman's tongue.

Cry for a nephew in the hills.
Cry for a nest among the rocks.
Let me sleep, and maybe dream
Of Rhoda's arms around me.

Πᾶσαν ἐγὼ τὴν νύκτα κινύρομαι· εὖτε δ' ἐπέλθῃ
ὄρθρος ἐλινῦσαι μικρὰ χαριζόμενος,
ἀμφιπεριτρύζουσι χελιδόνες, ἐς δέ με δάκρυ
βάλλουσιν, γλυκερὸν κῶμα παρωσάμεναι.
ὄμματα δ' οὐ λάοντα φυλάσσεται· ἡ δὲ Ῥοδάνθης
αὖθις ἐμοῖς στέρνοις φροντὶς ἀναστρέφεται.
ὦ φθονεραὶ παύσασθε λαλητρίδες· οὐ γὰρ ἔγωγε
τὴν Φιλομηλείην γλῶσσαν ἀπεθρισάμην·
ἀλλ' Ἴτυλον κλαίοιτε κατ' οὔρεα, καὶ γοάοιτε
εἰς ἔποπος κραναὴν αὖλιν ἐφεζόμεναι,
βαιὸν ἵνα κνώσσοιμεν· ἴσως δέ τις ἥξει ὄνειρος,
ὅς με Ῥοδανθείοις πήχεσιν ἀμφιβάλοι.

Damaskios

Zozime was a slave in body only.
Now, she has freed her body too.

Ζωσίμη, ἡ πρὶν ἐοῦσα μόνῳ τῳ σώματι δούλη,
καὶ τῷ σώματι νῦν εὗρεν ἐλευθερίην.

Tryphon

The musician Terpis met his end
Singing at banquets in Sparta.

No sword slew him, no flying rock.
As he sang, a fig in a food fight

Passed his lips and choked him.
Death never fails to find a way.

Τέρπης εὐφόρμιγγα κρέκων σκιάδεσσιν ἀοιδὰν
κάτθαν' †ενοστησας ἐν Λακεδαιμονίοις,
οὐκ ἄορι πληγείς, οὐδ' ἐν βέλει, ἀλλ' ἐνὶ σύκῳ
χείλεα. φεῦ· προφάσεων οὐκ ἀπορεῖ θάνατος.

Anonymous

Those cut off from sweet daylight I mourn no longer.
I weep for those living in constant fear of death.

Τοὺς καταλείψαντας γλυκερὸν φάος οὐκέτι θρηνῶ,
τοὺς δ' ἐπὶ προσδοκίῃ ζῶντας ἀεὶ θανάτου.

NOTES

Unless otherwise noted, all references are to *The Greek Anthology*, William Roger Paton, translator, Loeb Classical Library, Harvard University Press, Volumes I–V, cited by book and poem numbers.

I. Anonymous Epitaphs of No Known Date

Page 7: 7.155. The epitaph appears in the Anthology in a tract of poems attributed to Isidorus of Aegae, sixth century BCE. The actual century of its composition is uncertain.

Page 8: 7.309.

Page 9: Paul Friedländer, with Herbert B. Hoffleit, *Epigrammata: Greek Inscriptions in Verse from the Beginnings to the Persian Wars.* Ares Publishers, 1948, 1987, no. 80.

Page 10: Christopher W. Clairmont, *Gravestone and Epigram: Greek Memorials from the Archaic and Classical Period.* Verlag Philipp von Zabern, 1970, no. 23. This late-fifth-century BCE pillar is in the Kerameikos Museum in Athens.

Page 11: 7.621. *Sardinian celery: Ranunculus sardous.* According to the American poet Keith Waldrop, "a poisonous herb, whose bitter taste could draw the lips back in a grin or sarcastic snarl, *sardonic*, like a dog's." See *A Windmill Near Calvary*, University of Michigan Press, 1968, p. 21.

Page 12: 10.3.

Page 13: 7.342.

Page 14: 7.673.

Page 15: 11.442. Peisistratus reigned at Athens from 547 to 527 BCE.

The epitaph is said to have been inscribed on a statue of the tyrant at Athens. Page says the epitaph is not dateable (D. L. Page, *Further Greek Epigrams,* Cambridge University Press, 1981, p. 339).

Page 16: Friedländer, no. 135. This appears to be the oldest extant epitaph composed in elegiac couplets. Its four verses stood on a pillar along the main road running to Athens through the suburb of Sepolia. It seems to date from 575–550 BCE.

Page 17: Clairmont, no. 24, plate 12. Another very old example, the lines accompany a gravestone cameo depicting an exuberant horse and its youthful rider (perhaps about to be thrown).

Page 18: 7.325. *Sardanapallus:* The epitaph reads well on its own but rests on a complex allusion. In Greek legend, Sardanapallus, the last in a line of thirty kings of Assyria, was emblematic of the scandalous and slothful life. Herodotus, Ctesias, Diodorus Siculus, Aristophanes and others tell his story or allude to him. Aristotle cites him as an example of the lowest category of human existence, the "Life of Enjoyment," suitable only for beasts. In 682 BCE Sardanapallus's capital Nineveh was besieged. Two years into the siege, the Tigris River undermined his palace walls. Rather than live as a captive, he collected his wives and his treasure and set fire to them and himself.

Page 19: 7.84. The pre-Socratic Thales of Miletus (624–546 BCE) was the first Greek thinker to define general principles, set forth hypotheses, study electricity, and much else. Aristotle called him the first philosopher.

II. Late Archaic and Classical Periods

Page 27: 7.489.

Page 28: 7.153.

Page 29: 7.160.

Page 30: 7.226. *Abdera:* A coastal city in northeastern Greece, and the birthplace of Democritus.

Page 31: 7.677. The night before the battle, Megistias foretold his own death. The Spartan general Leonidas urged him to depart; Megistias sent away his only son but stayed with the army, and perished the next day. Forty years later, the historian Herodotus quotes this poem (Bk. 7.228) and tells us that Simonides, a friend of Megistias, had the epitaph set up at Thermopylae *in memoriam.*

Page 32: 7.248. The epitaph was inscribed on a monument dedicated to all the Greeks who fell while attempting to hold the pass against an invading Persian army at Thermopylae in 480 BCE. The size of the Persian army is exaggerated here ten times or more. The size of the Greek defense, which included about a thousand Spartan slaves, is accurate.

Page 33: 7.249. The epitaph was inscribed on a common monument to all those Spartans who fell while attempting to resist the invading Persian army at Thermopylae in 480 BCE. Leonidas, Sparta's king, led the allied Greeks. When an informer betrayed them, Leonidas remained with a small contingent in a heroic defense of the pass. All died. A hero cult was established at Sparta around this effort.

Page 34: 7.348.

Page 35: 7.507 (a).

Page 36: 7.254 (a).

Page 37: 7.280.

Page 38: 7.532.

Page 39: 7.346. *Sabinus:* Admiral of the Corinthian fleet.

Page 40: D. L. Page. *Further Greek Epigrams.* Cambridge University Press. 1981, 131.

Page 41: 7.265.

Page 42: 7.268. *Minos:* A legendary king of Crete, a great lawgiver, he was made a judge in Hades.

Page 43: 7.669.

III. Hellenistic Period

Page 52: 7.295.

Page 54: 7.665.

Page 55: 6.226.

Page 56: 7.740.

Page 57: 7.731.

Page 58: 7.655.

Page 59: 7.273.

Page 60: 7.283.

Page 61: 6.298. This satirical poem plays on a popular genre of dedicatory verse, in which professionals upon retirement dedicate the tools of their trade to an appropriate deity, hanging them up in the deity's temple. A soldier would hang his sword and shield in the temple of Ares, for example. In time, the genre developed an ironical turn: the old woman, once a beauty, dedicates her mirror to Aphrodite, etc. In Leonidas's poem, the ascetical Cynic has done without to the point of starvation. He cannot celebrate his "success," so Hunger does it for him, hanging his few belongings in a bush.

Page 62: 7.408.

Page 63: 7.452. *Eubulus:* The name of a fourth century BCE writer of comedies. In one fragment, he has Dionysus, the "god of wine," recommend restraint in drinking. The use of this name, here, may be a reference.

Page 64: 7.455.

Page 65: 7.170. *He's sleeping still:* The epitaph may have been carved into the base of a stone depicting a woman holding a child.

Page 66: 7.538.

Page 67: 7.202.

Page 68: 7.190.

Page 69: 7.215.

Page 70: 7.208.

Page 71: 7.212.

Page 72: 7.718.

Page 73: 7.414. *Rhinthon:* A third-century BCE author who specialized in so-called "satyr" plays. These often followed the performance of a tragic trilogy, providing an element of comic relief. Of his thirty-eight plays, fragments of eight survive, six of which are burlesques of tragedies by Euripides.

Page 74: 7.650.

Page 75: 7.415.

Page 76: 7.451.

Page 77: 7.447.

Page 78: 7.453.

Page 79: 7.471. The treatise mentioned here is Plato's *Phaido,* on the death of Socrates. One of the three charges for which the Athenian Assembly condemned Socrates to death was the corruption of youth.

Page 80: 7.454. The ancient Greeks considered it barbaric to drink undiluted wine. They had no beer or distilled spirits.

Page 81: 7.524. There are three voices here. The visitor queries the headstone, which replies once. The visitor then queries Charidas, the deceased, who replies four times. Pluto was god of the netherworld.

Page 82: 7.520.

Page 83: 7.728.

Page 84: 7.271.

Page 85: 7.277.

Page 86: 7.80. One poem survives by Heracleitus of Halicarnassus. See page 95.

Page 87: 7.544.

Page 88: 7.481.

Page 89: 7.735.

Page 90: 7.410.

Page 91: 7.276.

Page 92: 7.545. As this epitaph points out, the road to the Grecian underworld divided into a right-hand path that led good souls down to Elysium and a left-hand path for those less worthy, who went to sufferings in Tartarus. Hades' three judges, Minos, Rhadamanthus, and Aeacus, met the dead at a crossroads and passed judgment. See *The Odyssey* 4.564, Pindar's *Olympian Ode 2.75,* and Virgil's *Aeneid,* 6.540 ff., for various descriptions.

Page 93: 7.444.

Page 94: 7.499.

Page 95: 7.465.

Page 96: 7.315. *Timon:* A legendary misanthrope, often typecast in opposition to traditional Greek values. In the epitaphs especially, where friendship and sociability are routinely praised, Timon stands for the complete rejection of fellow human beings. Concerning his demise, the unspoken conclusion for a Greek may have been, "He won't be missed."

Page 97: 7.282.

Page 98: 7.546.

Page 99: 7.260.

Page 100: 7.533.

Page 101: 7.469.

Page 102: 7.721.

Page 103: 7.232.

Page 104: 7.8.

Page 106: 7.413. *Atalanta:* A mythic outdoorswoman famous for her speed. She raced Hippomenes, who distracted her by strewing golden apples in her way, winning the race and her hand in marriage.

Page 107: 7.173.

IV. The Millennium

Page 113: 7.543. Paton remarks: "Pliny (N.H. X.13) tells of ships being similarly sunk by flocks of quails alighting on them at night."

Page 114: 7.417 and 7.419. Meleager wrote several epitaphs for himself. This free version, by no means a line-for-line translation, is based on 7.417 but omits a few phrases, combining others from 7.419.

Page 116: 7.182.

Page 117: 7.482.

Page 118: 7.365.

Page 119: 7.299.

Page 120: 7.211.

Page 121: 7.400.

Page 122: 7.634.

Page 123: 7.399. *Sons of Oedipus:* The poem may describe a painting or refer to a pair of latter-day Greeks whose enmity resembled the legendary brothers cited here. In any case, the story being recalled concerns Oedipus's two sons, who, cursed by their father, went on wrangling even after death.

Page 124: 7.457.

Page 126: 7.376.

Page 127: 9.74. *Achaemenides and Menippus:* The two names reflect the extremes of society. The first signifies Persian royalty. The second was a common Greek name. Gow and Page date this anonymous piece by placing it, as here, between Antiphilus and Antipater of Thessalonica in the first century CE.

Page 128: 7.18. *Alcman:* Seventh-century BCE poet, author of the earliest choral lyrics. Alcman worked in Sparta but may have hailed from Sardis in present-day western Turkey. Except for a few fragments, his six books are lost.

Page 129: 7.398.

Page 130: 7.639.
Page 131: 7.402.
Page 132: 7.693.
Page 133: 7.378.
Page 134: 7.224.
Page 135: 7.381.
Page 136: 7.548.
Page 137: 11.159.
Page 138: 11.192.
Page 139: 11.264.
Page 140: 11.113.
Page 141: 7.394.
Page 142: 7.324.

V. Late Antiquity

Page 147: J. W. Mackail. *Select Epigrams from the Greek Anthology*. Longmans, Green, 1908, III.liv.

Page 148: 7.96. *The god was right to call you wise:* Apollo's oracle at Delphi told Socrates he was the wisest man in Greece.

Page 149: 7.744. The epitaph concerns a form of prophecy and fortune telling associated with bulls.

Page 150: 7.607.

Page 151: 10.82. Palladas wrote as a pagan in Byzantine Christian times. His theme here is the effeteness of an exhausted worldview.

Page 152: 7.582.

Page 153: 7.586.

Page 154: 7.576.

Page 155: 7.565.

Page 156: 9.677.

Page 157: 7.311. Answer to the riddle: Lot's wife.

Page 158: 5.237. "I didn't stop a dead young woman's tongue . . ." Jay explains the extended allusion succinctly: "The Thracian king Tereus, husband of Prokne, cut out the tongue of his sister-in-law, Philomela, to prevent her accusing him of having raped her. Prokne's revenge was to murder her young son by Tereus, Itylos, and to serve him to Tereus for dinner. Further disasters were averted by the gods, who intervened to turn Philomela into a nightingale, Prokne into a swallow, Itylos into a sandpiper, and Tereus into a hoopoe, a bird that nests among rocks" (Peter Jay, *The Greek Anthology,* rev. ed., Penguin Classics, 1981, p. 393). Here, the poet is telling the swallows of line 3 to trouble these others, victims of a violent mythic reality, and let him sleep with his fantasy, since he has brought no harm to the woman he loved.

Page 160: 7.553.

Page 161: 9.488.

Page 162: 11.282.

SELECTED BIBLIOGRAPHY

Texts

A. S. F. Gow and D. L. Page. *Hellenistic Epigrams.* 2 vols. Cambridge University Press, 1965.

——. *The Garland of Philip.* 2 vols. Cambridge University Press, 1968.

D. L. Page. *Further Greek Epigrams.* Cambridge University Press, 1981.

English-Language Translations

Richard Aldington. *The Poems of Meleager of Gadara.* Chatto & Windus: Phoenix Library, 1920.

——. *Medallions. From Anyte of Tegea, Meleager of Gadara, the Anacreontea, Latin Poets of the Renaissance.* Chatto & Windus, 1930.

Christopher W. Clairmont. *Gravestone and Epigram: Greek Memorials from the Archaic and Classical Period.* Verlag Philipp von Zabern, 1970.

Gordon L. Fain. *Ancient Greek Epigrams.* University of California Press, 2010.

Dudley Fitts. *Poems from the Greek Anthology.* New Directions, 1956.

Paul Friedländer, with Herbert B. Hoffleit. *Epigrammata: Greek Inscriptions in Verse from the Beginnings to the Persian Wars.* Ares Publishers, 1948, 1987.

Peter Jay. *The Greek Anthology.* Rev. ed. Penguin Classics, 1981.

J. W. Mackail. *Select Epigrams from the Greek Anthology.* Longmans, Green, 1908.

W. R. Paton. *The Greek Anthology.* 5 vols. Loeb Classical Library, Harvard University Press, 1917, 1993.

Kenneth Rexroth. *Poems from the Greek Anthology.* University of Michigan Press, 1962.

Robin Skelton. *Two Hundred Poems from the Greek Anthology.* University of Washington Press, 1971.

Criticism

M. Baumbach, A. Petrovic, and I. Petrovic, eds. *Archaic and Classical Greek Epigram.* Cambridge University Press, 2010.

Alan Cameron. *The Greek Anthology from Meleager to Planudes.* Oxford University Press. 1993.

Katharine Derderian. *Leaving Words to Remember: Greek Mourning and the Advent of Literacy.* Brill Academic Publishers, 2000.

Kathryn J. Gutzwiller. *Poetic Garlands: Hellenistic Epigrams in Context.* University of California Press, 1998.

Richmond Lattimore. *Themes in Greek and Latin Epitaphs.* University of Illinois, 1962.

Kenneth Rexroth. "The Greek Anthology," in *Classics Revisited.* New Directions. 1968.

Ann Suter. *Lament.* Oxford University Press, 2008.

Christos Tsagalis. *Inscribing Sorrow: Fourth Century Funerary Epigrams.* Walter de Gruyter, 2008.

BIOGRAPHIES OF THE POETS

AESCHYLUS 525–456 BCE. The earliest Greek playwright whose work survives, Aeschylus wrote more than eighty plays, of which seven remain. The transition in Athens from tyranny to democracy occurred during his youth. He fought in two major battles, Marathon and Salamis. Two epitaphs attributed to Aeschylus survive. His only son wrote plays as well.

AGATHIAS SCHOLASTICUS 536–582 CE. A Byzantine lawyer and scholar, Agathias studied in Alexandria and Constantinople. He wrote a history of the Emperor Justinian, compiled an anthology of contemporary poets, and produced many poems of his own. The Greek Anthology contains about 100 of his epigrams.

ANACREON One of the renowned early Greek lyric poets, Anacreon was born about 570 BCE in Ionia (present-day western Turkey). He served at court on the island of Samos and later in Athens, where he had many patrons. His songs were popular at symposia (drinking parties). His elegies and other poems were collected in five books. Only a few poems survive. Of the eighteen epigrams ascribed to him in the Anthology, many if not all are spurious.

ANTIPATER OF SIDON A Syrian in Rome in the late second century BCE. Cicero knew his work. He was famous for verse improvisations composed at the drop of a hat during parties. The Greek Anthology preserves at least 68 of his epigrams. Others may be his or written by another Antipater.

ANTIPATER OF THESSALONICA A poet writing between 20 BCE and

20 CE, this Antipater has ninety or more poems in the Anthology and is otherwise unknown. In fact, scholars have had a hard time distinguishing the poems of the two Antipaters, except by textual inference. His connection with Thessalonica is an educated guess. He may have taught rhetoric in Rome. He may have traveled in Asia.

ANTIPHILUS OF BYZANTIUM From Asia Minor, he flourished around 50 CE, possibly at the court of the Roman Emperor Nero. His work is prized for innovative phrasing.

ANYTE A third-century BCE Arcadian from Tegea, Anyte, like Leonidas and Nossis, was a major voice among the first generation of Hellenistic poets. Only her epigrams survive. She is famous for introducing rural themes into the genre. Later Greek poets admired her mastery of melody.

APOLLONIDES Probably from Asia Minor, references in some of his thirty-one epigrams place him on the millennial cusp between 6 BCE and 15 CE.

ARISTON Dates unknown. His three epigrams were collected by Meleager in the first century BCE.

CALLIMACHUS 300–240 BCE. Probably from Cyrene in Libya, Callimachus lived in Alexandria and is usually associated with the great library there, although his name is not on the list of its librarians. Perhaps the most influential poet of his time, he displayed an unusual economy of words. Surviving, in addition to sixty epigrams, are six hymns and fragments of some lyrics, satirical and occasional poems, elegies, and miniature epics (*epyllia*). Catullus translated his *Lock of Bereniké*. The Latin epigrammatist Martial extolled Callimachus and, like another poet, Sextus Propertius, was indebted to him. An advocate of compression, Callimachus declared the traditional epic obsolete. Though often embroiled in controversy, he appears to have been a sociable man who enjoyed some influence at the Greek court of the Ptolemies. His wife was Syracusan. He probably knew the pastoral poet Theocritus. Although culturally cosmopolitan, he may never have traveled beyond Egypt.

CARPHYLLIDES Nothing is certain about him, nor whether he lived before 90 BCE or as late as the second century CE.

Chaeremon Nothing is known about the author except that he lived between 300 and 100 BCE.

Cleoboulos A sixth-century BCE ruler of Lindos, a city on the island of Rhodes. Whether or not he was the true author of this poem remains in question.

Crinagoras of Mytilene 70 BCE–10 CE. An ambassador twice to Julius Caesar and to Augustus Caesar in Spain, Crinagoras, a Greek from the island of Lesbos, left fifty-one epigrams. He moved in Roman high society and wrote with a distinctive style of his life and times.

Damagetus A dozen of his epigrams are preserved in the Greek Anthology. Some of them indicate that Damagetus lived in the late third century BCE. Like Anyte, he seems to have been from the Peloponnese.

Damaskios Damaskios was head of the Neoplatonic academy in Athens when the Emperor Justinian shut it down in 529 CE as part of an attempt to expunge paganism from the Christianized Roman Empire. Damaskios went into exile in Persia but was pardoned later and returned to Athens. His highly regarded philosophical works are lost.

Diogenes Laertius A third-century CE author, he is best known for his biographical volume on the Greek philosophers. He wrote dozens of epitaphs on literary figures long dead. Others are in a comic or ironic vein.

Dionysius of Andros Nothing is known about this poet.

Dioscorides A late-third-century BCE poet, he left more than forty epigrams. He most likely lived in Alexandria, Egypt.

Diotimos Two poets go by this name in the Anthology. Nine of the eleven poems by one or the other were written before the first century BCE. Nothing certain can be said of either man.

Etruscus of Messene Early first century CE. In the Anthology, he is represented by one poem.

Hegesippus The themes and tone of his eight epigrams in the Anthology suggest that he wrote in the middle of the third century BCE. Otherwise, nothing is known about him.

Heracleitus The quality of his one preserved epigram warranted Callimachus's praise for this third-century BCE poet (see page 86).

Isidorus of Aegae The high quality and elegant style of the five preserved epigrams by this unknown poet argue for placing him in the Classical period.

Julianos, Prefect of Egypt Seventy poems are ascribed to this fifth-century CE governor.

Leonidas of Alexandria This first-century CE poet and astrologer specialized in trick verses. His patrons included the emperors Nero, Vespasian, and Domitian. Thirty of his forty poems in the Anthology are in couplets the letters of which, when assigned a numerical value, add up to the same sum. He also wrote several "echo" poems, another ingenious genre of questionable value.

Leonidas of Tarentum A third-century BCE poet associated with the city of Tarentum, Leonidas wrote more than 100 epigrams that have survived. They are mostly epitaphs and dedications. The Latin poets Virgil and Propertius regarded him highly and borrowed from him. His concern with working-class people is distinctive. He expanded the scope of the epigram in his day, as did his female contemporaries, Anyte and Nossis.

Lucilius A first-century CE grammarian patronized by Nero, he was a contemporary of Lucan and Petronius. Lucilius introduced humorous hyperbole into the epigram and influenced the great satiric Latin poet, Martial.

Meleager This first-century BCE poet and anthologist compiled a long-lived collection of epigrams containing work from the early seventh century to his own time. He was a masterful and prolific epigrammatist who influenced Catullus and the later Augustan poets, as well as the seventeenth-century English poet Robert Herrick.

Mnasalcas A third-century BCE poet who followed Anyte chronologically, and thematically too, especially in his many epitaphs on animals.

Nicarchus A satiric poet of the first century CE in the style of Lucilius.

Nicomachus Neither the poet nor the event this epitaph memorializes can be dated.

Nossis A third-century BCE poet from Locri on the southeastern tip of Italy, Nossis wrote in Doric Greek and was a near contemporary of Anyte. She may have written lyric poetry too, but, as with Anyte, only her epigrams survive. Her poems on love especially leave a strong personal impression.

PALLADAS OF ALEXANDRIA A late-fourth-century CE author, Palladas wrote more than 150 epigrams. His mood of pessimistic melancholy catches well the frame of mind of the latter-day Hellenist.

PHALAECUS A poet of the late fourth century BCE.

PHILETAS OF SAMOS Possibly the accomplished Philetas of Kos, a fourth-century BCE poet and tutor to both the ruler Ptolemy II and the great pastoral poet Theocritus. Ovid and Propertius considered him the equal of Callimachus as an elegist. Little of his work survives.

PHILLIP OF THESSALONICA A first-century CE poet and anthologist who published an anthology containing his and many others' epigrams, all composed after Meleager's collection.

PLATO Tradition holds that the philosopher and great prose stylist wrote verse as a young man. Of the epigrams ascribed to him, the quality is uniformly high.

POSIDIPPUS 310 BC–240 BC. A Macedonian adherent of Orphism, he lived at court on Samos and then for many years in Alexandria, at the court of Ptolemy I and II. A contemporary of Callimachus, he was a professional composer of epigrams and a prominent literary figure in his time. Twenty-six of his epigrams are in the Anthology. In 2001, 110 new epigrams were recovered from the wrappings of an Egyptian mummy. Twenty of them were epitaphs.

RHIANUS A third-century BCE Cretan poet and freedman, he wrote five epics and edited Homer. Ten epigrams survive in the Anthology.

SAPPHO The quintessential Greek lyric poet. Sappho's four surviving complete poems and many fragments are among the earliest examples in Western literature of an independent poetic voice. If, as most scholars hold, the epitaph on page 27 was written centuries later in the Hellenistic period, it is nonetheless Sapphic in expression.

SERAPION OF ALEXANDRIA There is only one poem ascribed to him in the Anthology. He wrote after 100 BCE and before 40 CE.

SIMONIDES Among the greatest of the Greek lyric poets, Simonides of Keos was born about 556 BCE and worked at courts in Athens and Thessaly. In his last years, he joined Pindar and Aeschylus at the court of Hiero in Syracuse. In stark simplicity and formal power his verse is unrivaled.

THEAETETUS Probably third century BCE. Three epigrams are ascribed to his name. Callimachus praises him elsewhere in the Anthology.

THEODORIDAS Late third century BCE. Seventeen epigrams are ascribed to him in the Anthology. He was probably from Sicily.

TRYPHON Nothing is known about this poet. His single collected epitaph appears very late, in a fifteenth-century CE collection. The story it tells probably concerns the seventh-century BCE poet Terpander.

TYMNES The author of seven extant epigrams, he is otherwise unknown. The name is Carian (a region in modern southwestern Turkey), not Greek. He must have written during or before the first century BCE.

ZONAS OF SARDIS An accomplished second- or first-century BCE poet, his sympathy with peoples to the east, with whom the Greeks warred, caused him political difficulties.